Another Republic

ANOTHER

REPUBLIC

17 European & South American Writers

Edited by Charles Simic & Mark Strand

The Ecco Press   New York City   1976

Library of Congress Cataloging in Publication Data
Main entry under title:
Another republic.
   Includes index.
   1. Literature, Modern—20th century—Translations into English.
2. English literature—Translations from foreign languages. I.
Simic, Charles, 1938-   . II. Strand, Mark, 1934-
PN6019.A5   808.81'04   76-16772
ISBN 0-912-94628-8

The following three pages constitute an extension of this copyright notice.

ACKNOWLEDGMENTS

YEHUDA AMICHAI: From *Poems* by Yehuda Amichai, translated from the Hebrew by Assia Gutmann, Copyright © 1968 by Yehuda Amichai; English translation Copyright © 1968 by Assia Gutmann; reprinted by permission of Harper & Row, Publishers, Inc.

JOHANNES BOBROWSKI: From *Shadow Land* by Johannes Bobrowski, English translation by Ruth and Matthew Mead, © Deutsche Verlags-Anstalt, Stuttgart, Germany; original title *Schattenland Ströme,* © Donald Carroll, London, 1966; reprinted by permission of Deutsche Verlags-Anstalt and André Deutsch Limited.

ITALO CALVINO: From *Invisible Cities* by Italo Calvino, translated by William Weaver; © 1972 by Guilio Einaudi Editore, s.p.a., © 1974 by Harcourt Brace Jovanovich, Inc.; reprinted by permission of Harcourt Brace Jovanovich, Inc.

PAUL CELAN: "Fugue of Death" translated by Christopher Middleton; all other poems translated by Michael Hamburger; © Deutsche Verlags-Anstalt, Stuttgart, Germany. Original title: *Mohn und Gedächtnis.* © Penguin Books, Baltimore, 1972.

JULIO CORTÁZAR: From *Cronopios and Fama,* by Julio Cortázar, translated by Paul Blackburn; Copyright © 1969 by Random House, Inc.; reprinted by permission of Pantheon Books, a Division of Random House, Inc.

JEAN FOLLAIN: From *Transparence of the World,* poems by Jean Follain, selected and translated by W. S. Merwin; translation Copyright © 1968, 1969 by W. S. Merwin; reprinted by permission of Atheneum Publishers.

Contents

Introduction

Another Republic is an attempt to call attention to certain tendencies and personalities in the poetry of Europe and South America that have influenced not only the work of the editors but that of an entire generation of American poets. The selection of poems is necessarily exclusive and not concerned with representing all the forces that have gone into the shaping of what is loosely referred to as "contemporary poetry." It is an experiment, a cosmology of a particular historical period—nothing more, nothing less.

Most of the poets included in *Another Republic* fall into two categories: the mythological and the historical. A few exist in between, partaking of both categories but resisting identification with either one. The poets whose impulse seems clearly mythological are Michaux, Ponge, Popa, Cortázar, Calvino, and Paz. Those whose impulse is historical are Amichai, Bobrowski, Celan, Herbert, Holub, Milosz, and Ritsos.

The origins of the mythological vision can be seen in surrealism, which, by concerning itself with the unconscious, found a method for uncovering and using archetypal imagery. It restored to the familiar world its strangeness and gave back to the poet his role of myth maker. Thus, for the mythological poet the miraculous is close at hand, easily encountered if he pays attention, as he must, since attention is his most important faculty. For him the poem is either a phenomenological interrogation, a process by which the archetype is dismantled, as in Ponge, or an elaborate narrative which tells the story of its own formation, as in Popa.

For the poets whose vision is dominated by historical consciousness, Cavafy is the great modern ancestor, since he understood perhaps better than any of his contemporaries that in history nothing changes except the names, that there are always victims, always oppressors. For poets like Milosz and Herbert there is no way to forget that despite our utopian ideologies we live in a world of wars, famine, and faithlessness. Such poets bear tragic witness to the social and political events of their time, and their work is characterized by two modes of self-expression: the lyric, which attempts to ennoble the suffering of those who are victimized or estranged; and the comic, which recognizes the absurdity of individual destinies in the presence of the great abstractions of history.

Another difference between the mythological poet and the poet of historical consciousness is that the first displays a greater interest in formal ideas while the second seems concerned primarily with content. For instance, it does not really matter what any poem of Ponge's is about; what counts is the way it is told. On the other hand, for Milosz the poem is pressured into being by the intensity of its message. This dichotomy, though never absolute, also accounts for the great difference in the voices of certain poets—the anonymity of the poet in Popa's poems, say, as contrasted with the presence in Celan's poems of his own voice.

Obviously, the characteristics mentioned above are not indigenous to any country or literary movement. They are international. And it is a sort of internationalism that binds these poets together. Coming right after the modernism of Pound, Eliot, Breton, Apollinaire, Alberti, and others—the old modernism with its extreme self-consciousness, its didacticism—the poets of *Another Republic* were able to take their own work more for granted. At no time do they apologize for their ability to consolidate and utilize the inventions of the older generation. And because of the great amount of translating that has been done in recent years more literature has been available to them than to any previous generation of writers. It is largely through translation that they know each other's work, and even manage to be influenced by it. Such a situation would render untrue Frost's dictum that poetry is what is lost in translation, for in fact it would seem that poetry is what is retained in translation.

Translation, of course, is what has made this book possible. All the poems in it are translations, yet have the authority of very good poems written originally in English. This is a tribute to the translators, but it says something too about the poem's ability to exist powerfully in a language other than the one in which it was written. How else are we to explain that there are young poets in the United States, say, whose work seems more influenced by the poems of Popa or Amichai than by those of Stevens, Eliot, or any other of their American forebearers? How else are we to account for the recent increase in the exchange of literary ideas and the growth of an international style which is dominant in poetry today?

For better or worse, an anthology acquires its character as much by the absence of certain well-known poets as by the inclusion of others as yet little known. It is hoped that the discoveries the reader makes will more than offset his disappointment at not finding, yet once again, poems he is already familiar with.

Because of the considerable attention Russian poets have received in this country we decided there was no use including them in this book. The same is true of poets like Neruda, Borges, Char, and others who, because they are considered major, have been translated many times and published widely. We have deliberately chosen poets who, for the most part, are not terribly well known, but who, we feel, are deserving of greater reputations. And our choice of individual poems has been determined solely by our enthusiasm for them. We hope our enthusiasm proves contagious.

C. S.
M. S.

Because *Another Republic* covers so short a historical period, the editors chose not to arrange the poets and their poems chronologically. They also chose against the impersonality of an alphabetical ordering. Instead, they chose an arrangement that reflects their taste and aesthetic judgment.

Another Republic

FRANCIS PONGE

The Pleasures of the Door

Kings do not touch doors.

They know nothing of this pleasure: pushing before one gently or brusquely one of those large familiar panels, then turning back to replace it—holding a door in one's arms.

. . . The pleasure of grabbing the midriff of one of these tall obstacles to a room by its porcelain node; that short clinch during which movement stops, the eye widens, and the whole body adjusts to its new surrounding.

With a friendly hand one still holds on to it, before closing it decisively and shutting oneself in—which the click of the tight but well-oiled spring pleasantly confirms.

Water

Below me, always below me is water. Always with lowered eyes do I look at it. It is like the ground, like a part of the ground, a modification of the ground.

It is bright and brilliant, formless and fresh, passive yet persistent in its one vice, gravity; disposing of extraordinary means to satisfy that vice—twisting, piercing, eroding, filtering.

This vice works from within as well: water collapses all the time, constantly sacrifices all form, tends only to humble itself, flattens itself on the ground, like a corpse, like the monks of certain orders. Always lower—that could be its motto; the opposite of excelsior.

*

One might almost say that water is mad, because of its hysterical need to obey gravity alone, a need that possesses it like an obsession.

Of course, everything in the world responds to this need, which always and everywhere must be satisfied. This cabinet, for example, proves to be terribly stubborn in its desire to stay on the ground, and if one day it found itself badly balanced, would sooner fall to pieces than run counter to that desire. But to a certain degree it teases gravity, defies it; does not give way in all its parts: its cornice, its moldings do not give in. Inherent in the cabinet is a resistance that benefits its personality and form.

LIQUID, by definition, is that which chooses to obey gravity rather than maintain its form, which rejects all form in order to obey gravity—and which loses all dignity because of that obsession, that pathological anxiety. Because of that vice—which makes it fast, flowing, or stagnant, formless or fearsome, formless *and* fearsome, piercingly fearsome in cases; devious, filtering, winding—one can do anything one wants with it, even lead water through pipes to make it spout out vertically so as to enjoy the way it collapses in droplets: a real slave.

The sun and the moon, however, are envious of this exclusive influence, and try to take over whenever water happens to offer the opening of great expanses, and above all when in a state of least resistance—spread out in shallow puddles. Then the sun exacts an even greater tribute: forces it into a perpetual cycle, treats it like a gerbil on a wheel.

*

Water eludes me . . . slips between my fingers. And even so! It's not even that clean (like a lizard or a frog): it leaves traces, spots, on my hands that are quite slow to dry or have to be wiped. Water escapes me yet marks me, and there is not a thing I can do about it.

Ideologically it's the same thing: it eludes me, eludes all definition, but in my mind and on this sheet leaves traces, formless marks.

*

Water's instability: sensitive to the slightest change of level. Running down stairs two at a time. Playful, childishly obedient, returning as soon as called if one alters the slope on this side.

The Pebble

The pebble is not an easy thing to define adequately.

If a simple description can satisfy, it could at once be said that it is a form or state of stone between a boulder and a grain of sand.

But this remark already implies a notion of stone that must be justified.

Let me not be reproached in this matter for going back even further than the flood.

*

All rocks are by scission issue of a single enormous ancestor. Of this fabulous body only one thing can be said, to wit that outside of limboes none still stands.

Reason finds it only amorphous and prevalent amidst the clammy reaches of the death pangs. It awakens for the baptism of a hero of the world's grandeur, but discovers the dreadful fix of a deathbed.

Let the reader not gloss over this too fast, but admire rather, instead of such heavy funereal expressions, the grandeur and glory of a truth which could, however little, render them transparent and not thereby seem altogether obscured.

So, on a planet already cold and dim, the sun shines now. No satellite aflame in its regard baffles any more. All the glory and all the existence, all that makes seeing and all that makes living, the source of all objective appearance is withdrawn from it. The heroes sprung from it, who revolved in its entourage, have been voluntarily eclipsed. But so that the truth for whose glory they abdicate— on behalf of its very source—preserve a public and objects, dead or on the point of being, they do not continue any less their round about it, their service as spectators.

You can imagine that such a sacrifice, the expulsion of life from natures once so glorious and ardent, would not have occurred without some dramatic inner reversals. This is the origin of Earth's gray chaos, our humble and magnificent abode.

So, after a period of twists and turns like those of a body tossing in sleep under covers, our hero, mated (by his consciousness) as by a monstrous straitjacket, knew no more than intimate explosions, more and more rare, with a shattering effect upon a more and more heavy and cold envelope.

The one dead and the other chaotic are now confounded.

*

The history of this body once and for all having lost along with the faculty of being moved that of being recast as one complete individual, since the slow catastrophe of cooling off, will be no more than that of a perpetual disintegration. But it is at this moment that other things occur: grandeur dead, life makes clear at once that it has nothing in common with it. At once, in countless ways.

Such is the globe's appearance today. The cadaver in pieces of the creature of the world's grandeur does no more than serve as decor for the life of millions of beings infinitely smaller and more ephemeral than it. Their thronging is in places so dense that it conceals completely the sacred skeleton which not long ago served them as unique support. And it is only an infinity of their cadavers which, succeeding from then on in imitating the consistency of stone, by what is called plant soil, permits them for a few days to reproduce themselves without owing anything to rock.

Incidentally the liquid element, of an origin perhaps as ancient as the one I am treating here, having been assembled over more or less great expanses, covers it up, rubs up against it, and by repeated blows hastens its erosion.

I shall describe then some of the forms that stone, sparse now and humiliated by the world, reveals to our eyes.

*

The biggest fragments, slabs almost invisible under the intertwined vegetations that cling there as much by religion as for other motives, constitute the global skeleton.

These are veritable temples: not just constructions erected arbitrarily upon the ground, but the impassive remains of the ancient hero who was not too long ago veritably in the world.

Engaged in imagining great things amid the shadow and fragrance of the forests that sometimes conceal these mysterious blocks, man by wit alone supposes underneath their continuity.

In the same places numerous smaller blocks draw your attention. Sown about under woods by Time, uneven balls of crumbled stone, molded by the dirty fingers of this god.

Since the explosion of their enormous ancestor, and their trajectory through heaven brought down beyond resurgency, the boulders have been silent.

Encroached upon and fractured by germination, like a man who no longer shaves, furrowed and filled up by loose earth, none of them—incapable now of any reaction—any longer says one word.

Their shapes, their bodies crack. In the wrinkles of experience naïveté comes on and settles down. Roses sit on their gray knees, and harangue them in their naïve way. They let them. They whose disastrous hail once cleared forests and whose duration is eternal in its stupor and resignation.

They smile to see around them roused up and condemned so many generations of flowers, of a flesh tint besides—no matter that it may be said scarcely more alive than theirs—and of a flush as pale and faded as their gray. They think (as statues do that never bother to say so) that these tints are borrowed from the light in the skies at sundown, light itself tried on by the skies every evening in memory of a far more splendid fire when, from that famous cataclysm on the occasion of which hurled violently into the air, they knew a magnificent hour of liberty brought to an end by this tremendous crash. Not far off, the sea at the rocky knees of the giant spectators on its shores, from the foaming efforts of their stricken women, ceaselessly rips up blocks that it guards, embraces, cradles, coddles, resifts, kneads, caresses, and polishes in its arms against its body or abandons in a corner of its mouth like a Sucret, then pushes from her mouth again and sets down upon a hospitable, gently sloping shore amidst an already numerous flock within her reach, with a view to picking it up again soon so as to attend to it more affectionately, passionately yet.

Meanwhile the wind blows. It makes the sand fly. And if one of these particles, the final and most minute form of the object concerning us, happens to really get into our eyes, it is thus that stone, in its peculiarly dazzling way, punishes and terminates our contemplation.

Nature thus closes our eyes just when the time has come to examine our memory and ask whether the information accumulated by extended contemplation there would not have already provided it with some principles.

*

To a mind that is easy prey to ideas encouraged at once by such appearances, in regard to stone nature will finally appear, perhaps in too simple a light, like a watch whose principle consists of wheels turning at quite varying speeds, although they are activated by a single engine. Plants, animals, gases, and liquids, in dying and in being born again, revolve in a more or less rapid fashion. The great wheel of stone seems to us practically immobile and, even theoretically, we can understand only a part of the phase of its very slow disintegration.

So much so that contrary to common opinion which holds it in the eyes of man as a symbol of endurance and impassivity, you can say in fact that stone, never re-forming in nature, is in reality the only thing in it that dies constantly.

So that when life, through the mouth of beings who receive successively from it and for a rather short period the detritus, leads us to believe that it envies the indestructible solidity of the scene that it inhabits, in reality it assists in the continuous disintegration of this scene. And here is the unity that appears dramatic to it: it thinks confusedly that its support may one day fail it, while it itself feels eternally revivable. In a scene which has given up being moved, and thinks only of falling in ruins, life becomes anxious and agitated at being able only to revive.

It is true that stone itself at times looks agitated. It is in its last stages, when as pebbles, gravel, sand, dust, it is no longer capable of playing its role as container and support for animate things. Out of control of the fundamental block it rolls, it flies, it claims a place on the surface again, and all life then draws far back from the dreary expanses where the frenzy of despair alternately disperses and reassembles it.

I will remark finally, as a very important principle, that all forms of stone, which all represent some state of its evolution, exist in the world simultaneously. Here no generations, no races have vanished. Temples, Demigods, Miracles, Mammoths, Heroes, Ancestors every day live next to their grandchildren. Each man can as flesh and bone touch all the possibles of this world in his garden. No conception: all exists; or rather, as in paradise, all conception exists.

*

If now I want to examine more attentively one particular type of stone, the perfection of its form, the fact that I can hold it and turn it about in my hand, makes me choose the pebble.

Also too, the pebble is the stone exactly at the period when the age of the person, of the individual, begins for it; that is to say, of the word. Compared to the rocky bank from which it directly derives, it is stone already fragmented and polished in a very large number of almost similar individuals. Compared to the smallest piece of gravel it can be said that by the place where it is found, since man also hasn't customarily made any practical use of it, it is still wild stone, or at least not domestic.

For some time yet meaningless in any practical order of the world, let's profit from its virtues.

*

Borne one day by one of the innumerable carts of the flood, which since then, it seems, only discharge now for our ears their vain freight, each pebble rests upon the pile of forms of its ancient state, and forms of its future.

Not far from the places where a bed of plant soil still conceals its enormous ancestors, at the base of rocky bank where the act of love of its immediate parents occurs, it has its seat in the ground shaped by the seed of the same, where the earthworking flood searches for and loses it.

But these places where the sea ordinarily relegates it are the most improper for homologation. Its populations rest there to the knowledge of the one expanse only. Each one thinks itself lost there because it has no number and because it sees only blind forces taking account of it.

And indeed everywhere such flocks rest, they practically cover the whole ground and their back forms a clumsy area for the foot to move over or the mind.

No birds. Blades of grass at times arise from them. Lizards cross them, skirt them naturally. Grasshoppers leaping measure themselves rather between them than they measure them. Men sometimes will toss one of theirs listlessly away.

But these last few objects, lost in disorder amidst a solitude broken into by dry grass, seawrack, old corks and all sorts of debris of human provisions,—imperturbable amid the strongest whirls of the atmosphere,—are mute spectators at the show of these forces that run blindly to the point of breathlessness chasing everything beyond all reason.

However, attached nowhere, they remain in whatever their place may be on the expanse. The strongest wind that can uproot a tree or demolish an edifice cannot displace a pebble. But as dust is tossed around, so too sometimes the ferrets of the hurricane unearth one of those boundary marks of chance from whatever their locations for centuries under the opaque and temporal bed of sand.

*

But on the other hand water, which makes slippery and communicates its fluid quality to all that it can completely wrap, sometimes manages to seduce these forms and drag them off. For the pebble remembers that it was born by the effort of this shapeless monster on the equally shapeless monster of stone. And as its person still can be achieved only by several applications of the liquid, it remains forever docile to it by definition.

Dull on the ground, as day is dull in relation to night, at the very instant that the wave picks it up again it polishes it. And although the wave doesn't operate at depth, and only barely penetrates the very fine and close-grained agglomerate, the very thin though very active adherence of the liquid causes an obvious modification on its surface. It seems that it repolishes it, and thus itself dresses the wounds made by their previous amours. Then, for a moment, the pebble's exterior resembles its interior: it has over all its body the look of youth.

However, its form when perfect supports both milieus. It remains imperturbable in the disorder of the seas. It comes out of it only smaller, but entire, and if you will as *great*, since its proportions do not in any way depend upon its volume.

Removed from the liquid it dries at once. That is, despite the monstrous efforts to which it has been submitted, no liquid trace will remain on its surface: it is shed without any effort.

In the end, smaller from day to day but always sure of its form, blind, solid, and dry at core, its character thus is not allowed to be confused but simply reduced by the waters. So, when—beaten—it is finally sand, water doesn't penetrate it exactly as it would dust. Keeping then all the traces, except precisely those of the liquid, which limits itself to being able to efface upon it those that others make, it lets pass through it the whole sea, which is lost in its depth without in any way being able to turn it into mud.

*

I'll say no more of it, for this idea of signs disappearing makes me reflect upon the faults of a style that leans too much upon words.

Too happy only to have for these beginnings known enough to have chosen *the pebble*: for a man of wit can only smile, but doubtlessly he will be touched, when my critics say: "Having undertaken to write a description of stone, he found himself weighed under it."

The Horse

Many times the size of man, the horse has flaring nostrils, round eyes under half-closed lids, cocked ears and long muscular neck.

The tallest of man's domestic animals, and truly his designated mount.

Man, somewhat lost on an elephant, is at his best on a horse, truly a throne to his measure.

We will not do away with the horse, I hope?

He will not become a curiosity in a zoo?

. . . Already now, in town, he is no more than a miserable sub-
stitute for the automobile, the most miserable means of traction.

Ah, the horse is also—does man suspect it?—something else
besides! He is *impatience* nostrilized.

His weapons are running, biting, bucking.

He seems to have a keen nose, keen ears, and very sensitive eyes.

The greatest tribute one can pay him is having to fit him with
blinders.

But no weapon . . .

Whereby the temptation to add one. One only. A horn. Thereby
the unicorn.

The horse, terribly nervous, is aerophagous.

Hypersensitive, he clamps his jaws, holds his breath, then re-
leases it, making the walls of his nasal cavities vibrate loudly.

That is why this noble beast, who feeds on air and grass alone,
produces only straw turds and thunderous fragrant farts.

Fragrant thunderisms.

What am I saying, feeds on air? Gets drunk on it. Sniffs it, savors
it, snorts it.

He rushes into it, shakes his mane in it, kicks up his hind legs
in it.

He would evidently like to fly up in it.

The flight of clouds inspires him, urges him to imitation.

He does imitate it: he tosses, prances . . .

And when the whip's lightning claps, the clouds gallop faster
and rain tramples the earth. . . .

Out of your stall, high-spirited over-sensitive armoire, all polished
and smoothed!

Great beautiful period piece!

Polished ebony or mahogany.

Stroke the withers of this armoire and immediately it has a
faraway look.

Dust cloth at the lips, feather mop at the rump, key in the lock
of the nostrils.

His skin quivers, irritably tolerating flies, his shoe hammers the ground.

He lowers his head, leans his muzzle toward the ground and consoles himself with grass.

A stepstool is needed to look on the upper shelf.

Ticklish skin, as I was saying . . . but his natural impatience is so profound, that inside his body the parts of his skeleton behave like pebbles in a torrent!

Seen from the apse, the highest animal nave in the stable . . .

Great saint! Great horse! Beautiful behind in the stable . . .

What is this splendid courtesan's behind that greets me, set on slim legs, high heels?

Giant goose of the golden eggs, strangely clipped.

Ah, it is the smell of gold that assails my nostrils!

Leather and manure mixed together.

Strong-smelling omelette, from the goose of the golden eggs.

Straw omelette, earth omelette, flavored with the rum of your urine, dropping from the crack under your tail . . .

As though fresh from the oven, on a pastry sheet, the stable's rolls and rum balls.

Great saint, with your Byzantine eyes, woeful, under the harness . . .

A sort of saint, humble monk at prayer, in the twilight.

A monk? What am I saying? . . . A pontiff, on his excremental palanquin! A pope—exhibiting to all comers a splendid courtesan's behind, generously heart-shaped, on slender legs ending elegantly in high-heeled shoes.

WHAT IS THIS CLACKING OF THE BIT?

THESE DULL THUDS IN THE STALL?

WHAT'S GOING ON?

PONTIFF AT PRAYER?

SCHOOLBOY IN DETENTION?

GREAT SAINTS! GREAT HORSES (HORSES OR HEROES?), OF THE

BEAUTIFUL BEHIND IN THE STABLE,
WHY, SAINTLY MONK, ARE YOU WEARING RIDING BREECHES?
—INTERRUPTED DURING HIS MASS, HE TURNED HIS BYZANTINE
EYES TOWARD US. . . .

HENRI MICHAUX

I am writing to you
from a far-off country

1

We have here, she said, only one sun in the month, and for only
a little while. We rub our eyes days ahead. But to no purpose.
Inexorable weather. Sunlight arrives only at its proper hour.

Then we have a world of things to do, so long as there is light,
in fact we hardly have time to look at one another a bit.

The trouble is that nighttime is when we must work, and we
really must: dwarfs are born constantly.

2

When you walk in the country, she further confided to him, you
may chance to meet with substantial masses on your road. These
are mountains and sooner or later you must bend the knee to
them. Resisting will do no good, you could go no farther, even by
hurting yourself.

I do not say this in order to wound. I could say other things if
I really wanted to wound.

3

The dawn is gray here, she went on to tell him. It was not always like this. We do not know whom to accuse.

At night the cattle make a great bellowing, long and flutelike at
the end. We feel compassionate, but what can we do?

The smell of eucalyptus surrounds us: a blessing—serenity, but
it cannot protect us from everything, or else do you think that it
really can protect us from everything?

4

I add one further word to you, a question rather.

Does water flow in your country too? (I don't remember
whether you've told me so) and it gives chills too, if it is the real
thing.

Do I love it? I don't know. One feels so alone when it is cold. But quite otherwise when it is warm. Well then? How can I decide? How do you others decide, tell me, when you speak of it without disguise, with open heart?

5

I am writing to you from the end of the world. You must realize this. The trees often tremble. We collect the leaves. They have a ridiculous number of veins. But what for? There's nothing between them and the tree any more, and we go off troubled.

Could not life continue on earth without wind? Or must everything tremble, always, always?

There are subterranean disturbances, too, in the house as well, like angers which might come to face you, like stern beings who would like to wrest confessions.

We see nothing, except what is so unimportant to see.

Nothing, and yet we tremble. Why?

6

We women here all live with tightened throats. Do you know, although I am very young, in other days I was still younger, and my companions were too. What does that mean? There is surely something horrible in it.

And in other days when, as I have already told you, we were younger still, we were afraid. Someone might have taken advantage of our confusion. Someone might have said to us: "You see, we're going to bury you. The moment has arrived." We were thinking: "It's true, we might just as well be buried this evening, if it is definitely stated that this is the moment."

And we did not dare run too much: Out of breath, at the end of a race, arriving in front of a ditch all prepared, and no time to say a word, no breath.

Tell me, just what is the secret in regard to this?

7

There are constantly, she told him further, lions in the village, who walk about without any hindrance at all. On condition that we pay no attention to them, they pay no attention to us.

But if they see a young woman running in front of them, they have no desire to apologize for her anxiety. No! They devour her at once.

That is why they constantly walk about the village where they have nothing to do, for quite obviously they might yawn just as well elsewhere.

8

For a long, long time, she confided to him, we have been in combat with the sea.

On the very rare occasions when she is blue, soft, one might suppose her to be happy. But that would not last. Her smell says so anyway, a smell of rot (if it is not her bitterness).

Here I should explain the matter of the waves. It is terribly complicated, and the sea . . . I implore you, have confidence in me. Would I want to deceive you? She is not only a word. She is not only a fear. She exists; I swear it to you; one sees her constantly.

Who? Why, we, we see her. She comes from far away to wrangle with us and to terrify us.

When you come you will see for yourself, you will be very startled. "Well, I'll be. . . !" you'll say, for she is stupefying.

We'll look at her together. I am sure I will not be afraid. Tell me, will this never happen?

9

I cannot have you with a doubt, she continues, with a lack of confidence. I should like to speak to you again of the sea. But the obstacle remains. The streams go forward; but not she. Listen, don't be angry, I swear it to you, I wouldn't dream of deceiving you. She is like that. No matter how excited she gets, she will halt before a little sand. She's a great falterer. She would certainly like to go forward, but there's the story.

Later on, maybe, some day she will go forward.

10

We are more than ever surrounded by ants, says her letter. They push the dust uneasily at top speed. They take no interest in us.

Not one raises its head.

This is the most tightly closed society that could exist, although outdoors they spread out constantly in all directions. No matter, their projected schemes, their preoccupations . . . they are among themselves . . . everywhere.

And up to the present time not one has raised its head toward us. It would rather be crushed.

11

She writes to him again:

You cannot imagine all that there is in the sky, you would have to see it to believe it. So now, the . . . but I'm not going to tell you their name at once.

In spite of their air of weighing a great deal and of occupying almost all the sky, they do not weigh, huge though they are, as much as a newborn baby.

We call them clouds.

It is true that water comes out of them, but not by compressing them, or by pounding them. It would be useless, they have so little.

But, by reason of their occupying lengths and lengths, widths and widths, deeps also and deeps, and of puffing themselves up, they succeed in the long run in making a few droplets of water fall, yes, of water. And we are really wet. We run off furious at having been trapped; for nobody knows the moment when they are going to release their drops; sometimes they rest for days without releasing them. And one would stay home waiting for them in vain.

12

The education regarding chills is not well handled in this country. We are ignorant of the true rules and when the event appears, we are taken unawares.

It is Time, of course. (Is it the same with you?) One must arrive a little sooner than it does; you see what I mean, only a tiny little bit ahead. You know the story of the flea in the drawer? Yes, of course. And how true it is, don't you think! I don't know what more to say. When are we going to see each other at last?

Icebergs

Icebergs, without guardrail, without girdle, where old weather-beaten cormorants and the souls of recently dead sailors lean on their elbows on the enchanting and hyperboreal nights.

Icebergs, Icebergs, cathedrals without religion of the eternal winter, robed in the glacial skullcap of the planet Earth.

How high, how pure are your edges, born of the cold.

Icebergs, Icebergs, back of the North Atlantic, august Buddhas frozen on uncontemplated seas, gleaming Lighthouses of Death without issue, the desperate cry of the silence lasts for centuries.

Icebergs, Icebergs, Solitaries without cause, countries barred-up, distant and free of vermin. Parents of islands, parents of springs, how well I see you, how familiar you are to me. . . .

From In the Land of Magic

1

The hunchback? A poor wretch, unconsciously obsessed by paternity (sexually rather high-strung, as we know, but paternity is what itches him most, they claim).

To comfort him they draw out of his hump another hunchback, a very little one.

What a strange tête-à-tête, when they look at each other for the first time, the old one comforted, the other already bitter and loaded with the extreme dejection of the infirm.

The hunchbacks whom one draws out for them are not true hunchbacks, needless to say, nor really offspring, nor really alive. They disappear after several days without leaving any traces.

But the hunchback has got a grip on himself, and that is not the least of miracles.

Of course shock is indispensable. Shock is what chiefly counts; the galvanization of the individual, who at first is all a-tremble from it.

On the other hand, if the hunchback looks with indifference at the little creature drawn from his hump, the effort is wasted.

You can draw two dozen out of him without any effect, without the slightest improvement in him.

What to make of it? You have there a true, perfect hunchback.

2

Suddenly you feel a touch. But nothing is really visible beside you, especially if the day is no longer perfectly clear, at the end of the afternoon (the time when *they* come out).

Birth

Pon was born of an egg, then he was born of a codfish and while being born made it explode, then he was born of a shoe through bipartition, the smaller shoe being at the left and he at the right, then he was born of a rhubarb leaf at the same time as a fox; the fox and he looked at each other a second then made off each in his own direction. Next he was born of a bedbug, of a lobster's eye, of a bottle; of a sea lion, and he came out of it through the mustaches, of a tadpole and he came out of it through its behind, of a mare and he came out through the nostrils, then he shed tears searching for the teats, for he had come to the world only to suck. Then he was born of a trombone and the trombone nursed him for thirteen months, then he was weaned and entrusted to the sand which stretched everywhere for this was the desert. And none but the son of the trombone can nourish himself in the desert, none but he and the camel, then he was born of a woman and greatly surprised, and, reflecting upon her breast, he kept sucking, he kept spitting out he no longer knew what, he noted next that this was a woman although nobody had ever made the slightest allusion to this subject to him, he began to raise his head, all by himself, to look at her with a perspicacious little eye, but the perspicacity was only a glimmer, the astonishment was very much greater and, considering his age, his great pleasure was still to make glub glub glub, and to nestle upon her breast, that lovely window pane, and to suck again and again.

He was born of a zebra, he was born of a sow, he was born of a stuffed monkey, one leg fastened to a mock cocoa tree and the other hanging down, he came out smelling all over of oakum, and began making a lot of noise and whistling in the office of the naturalist who rushed at him with the obvious intention of stuffing him, but he escaped from him and was born in perfect silence of a foetus which was at the bottom of a glass jar, he came out of it through the head, an enormous spongy head, softer than a uterus, where for more than three weeks he let matters simmer, then he was born rapidly of a live mouse, for he had to hurry, the naturalist having got wind of something; then he was born of a shell which exploded in the air; then feeling himself still observed, he managed to be born of a frigate bird and passed the ocean under his feathers, then in the first island come to he was born into the first thing come upon and this was a turtle, but as he grew up he noticed that it was the wheel hub from an old-style hackney coach brought there by Portuguese planters. Then he was born of a cow, which is nicer, then of a giant lizard of New Guinea, big as a donkey, then he was born for the second time of a woman, and in the course of that was mindful of the future, it was women after all whom he knew best and with whom he would be most at ease later, and now he was already looking at that breast so soft and full, while making the little comparative judgments which his already considerable experience permitted.

From The Emanglons

Manners and Customs

1

Without any apparent cause an Emanglon will suddenly start to weep, maybe because he sees a leaf or some light object trembling, or a mote falling, or a leaf falling in his memory, grazing on other recollections, varied and distant ones, maybe because his destiny as a man, appearing inside him, makes him suffer.

People don't ask for explanations. They understand and out of sympathy they turn away from him to put him at his ease.

But, since they are frequently beset by a kind of collective decrystallization, groups of Emanglons, if this should happen at the café, start to weep silently, tears drown their eyes, the room and tables disappear from sight. Conversations remain suspended with nobody to bring them to an end. A kind of internal thaw, accompanied by chills, takes hold of them. But gently. For what they feel is a general crumbling of the limitless world, and not of their mere selves or of their past, against which nothing, nothing can be done.

They enter, and well for them that they sometimes enter the Great Current, the vast and desolate Current.

At these moments the Emanglons are without antennae, but moving underneath.

Then, when the thing passes, they take up, although softly, their conversations, without ever alluding to the invasion they have undergone.

2

Music is discrete there. The musicians even more so. They do not let themselves be seen while they play.

One day one of them, who was playing in the drawing room, supposing that I was watching him, almost strangled himself for shame; but I had not even heard him—he was playing so softly.

Their music with its dying sounds always seems to be coming through a mattress. That's what they like: tenuous sounds, coming from nobody knows where, fading out every second, trembling and uncertain melodies, which finish off, however, in great harmonic surfaces—wide layers suddenly outspread.

They like still better the impression that the music is moving about (as if the musicians were winding around a mountain or following a twisting narrow lane), moving about and coming to them as if by chance from the echoes and the winds.

3

At the theater they reveal their taste for the remote. The hall is long, the stage deep.

The images, the forms of the characters appear there, by means of a play of mirrors (the actors perform in another hall), appear more real there than if they were present, more concentrated, purged, definite, unburdened of the halo which a personal appearance always gives them.

Some words, that come from the ceiling, are spoken in their names.

The impression of fate, without the shadow of pathos, is extraordinary.

4

The sick person who does not suffer from chaotic respiration is taken care of, and I saw some cured whom I had previously found in bad shape.

Their first remedy is to knock him unconscious by striking his head a telling blow with a stick. (A man must remain outside his disease.) Then comes the treatment. They have extracts from a great many plants in their pharmacopia. Of course! Like every other place. But these scarcely count.

Above all else they turn over to a dog the responsibility for curing him. As soon as they've managed to shut a dog into the patient's room, they happily disperse. The latter is, if I may say so, in good hands. In just one night, sometimes, he finds he is cured. It is a fact that the dog's presence brings him a salutary rest.

If the dog will not consent to remain sleeping on the bed: a bad sign, though not absolutely hopeless. It is normal for the disease to begin by triumphing. But if on the second and third nights the animal seeks to get out, to dig under the door, it's all over, the patient is done for; as well close his mouth immediately.

If the dog does not bark and remains quiet, the patient is in no danger, but still he may be no more than the shadow of himself from now on. *No man has ever died beside a sleeping dog.* The dog always wakes up in time to bark. The barking is naturally meaningful. As soon as you've heard it, you can shut the patient's mouth. It is your duty, even.

A girl is hurriedly summoned, and even if it is nighttime and very stormy she must come in her fine clothes and with face painted the colors of health and happiness. Now it is her turn to act. The doctors cork up their bottles and depart with the dog.

5

If, while an Emanglon is home entertaining somebody, a fly comes into the room where they are, the guest, even if he is his best friend, will get up and leave at once without saying a word, wearing that ruffled and stung expression which is inimitable. The other has understood, even if he has seen nothing. Only a fly could cause this disaster. Drunk with hatred, he searches for it. But his friend is already far away.

Emanglons cannot endure living in the same room with a fly. In their eyes the cohabitation has something monstrous about it. They feel deeply wounded, but more than that, diminished, depressed, and some have been seen who could barely drag themselves out of doors.

The great treachery is to enter the home of someone you intend to injure, provided with a fly hidden in your pocket, to let it loose in the dining room and then to act the part of the man who has been insulted. But the other has his eye on you, you may be sure! He watches your pockets, your collar, your sleeves, he suspects immediately that there's a fly in this visit. So you must act prudently. As in everything else, you must be skillful, and if you get a good chance, don't think that your work is over with.

It was during the great speech of Orname, the minister, that a fly was let loose in the hall to reduce him to helplessness and upset the assembly. The fly was so ingenuous as to alight on his nose.

The great man very coolly caught it, put it in a box, and went on with his speech.

Then he had the audacity to have the fly handed around in a closed box among the deputies, so that its owner could reclaim it. But all, Emanglons to the core, bent over it placidly, each in his turn, without giving himself away.

The Enanglom

This is an animal without shape, the strongest of all, three-fourths of him muscles, and all muscles in his outside layer, which is nearly a foot thick all over. He is built to scale any rocks, even sheer ones.

His skin, which is so amorphous, becomes grappling hooks.

No animal attacks him; too high off the ground for a rhinoceros to be able to crush, he would be more likely to overthrow it, for he has everything but speed.

The tigers would break their claws without cutting his skin; even a flea or a gadfly, a cobra, finds no sensitive place in him.

And although he is wonderfully aware of all that is happening around him, except, it seems, at midsummer, no feeling can be found in him.

He sits down in the water to feed; a bubbling and especially a great swirling of water accompanies him and perfectly intact fish come to the surface to float with stomachs in the air.

Deprived of water, he dies; the rest is mystery.

It is not unheard of for people to find crocodiles shattered to pieces on the banks of the rivers he frequents.

JEAN
FOLLAIN

The Egg

The old woman dried an egg
with her working apron
heavy egg the color of ivory
which nobody claims from her
then she looks at the autumn
through the little dormer
and it is like a fine painting
the size of a picture book
nothing is
out of season
and the fragile egg
that she holds in her palm
remains the one thing that is new.

The Barn Owl

They say that the barn owl
drinks the oil of the sanctuary lamps
in the village churches;
she comes in through a broken pane
during the night hours
when the good and the violent are sleeping
when pride and love are worn out
when the foliage dreams.
The beast warms her blood
with the virgin light-giving oil.

Black Meat

Around stones called precious
which only their own
dust can wear down
the eaters of venison
carve in silence
their black meat
the trees on the horizon
imitate in outline
a giant sentence.

Housewives

Housewives as the nights came in
said they'd done nothing with the day
and on his bed the man dying
heard them;
one spoke in a crystalline voice
and her body with its grave beauty
carried in its arms a child
in a bib with faded ribbons
coughing at the gusts of smoke
from the weeds burning
in a silent garden.
Having long aired their complaints
until the last bird song
they separated at last
to salt
their evening broth.

Father and Daughter

She was born in the midst of the black frock coats
of the doctors who performed the caesarean,
her mother died,
her father kept his thunderous voice,
he gripped in his long fingers
the edges of tables ruled in gold
during his discussions with the cardinals;
alone at times he groaned
covered with patches of light by the setting sun
and with his cuff out of his sleeve
his glances would wander over the Chinese vases
but his daughter
at no time made much noise
by the long windows she sewed
haloed in the color of the day
her fingers with their desireless nails
gathered light fabrics
which she tore with her teeth.

Signs

Sometimes when a customer in a shadowy restaurant
is shelling an almond
a hand comes to rest on his narrow shoulder
he hesitates to finish his glass
the forest in the distance is resting under its snows
the sturdy waitress has turned pale
he will have to let the winter night fall
has she not often seen
on the last page
of a book of modest learning
the word end printed
in ornate capitals?

Asia

Through the window of the school
the map of Asia could be seen
Siberia was as warm as India
the insects made their way
from the Indus to the Amour River;
at the foot of the wall
a man was eating his soup
which the beans had turned mauve
he was grave
and alone in the world.

ZBIGNIEW HERBERT

Wooden Die

A wooden die can be described only from without. We are therefore condemned to eternal ignorance of its essence. Even if it is quickly cut in two, immediately its inside becomes a wall and there occurs the lightning-swift transformation of a mystery into a skin.

For this reason it is impossible to lay foundations for the psychology of a stone ball, of an iron bar, of a wooden cube.

Study of the Object

1

The most beautiful is the object
which does not exist

it does not serve to carry water
or to preserve the ashes of a hero

it was not cradled by Antigone
nor was a rat drowned in it

it has no hole
and is entirely open

seen
from every side
which means
hardly anticipated

the hairs
of all its lines
join
in one stream of light

neither
blindness
nor
death
can take away the object
which does not exist

2

mark the place
where stood the object
which does not exist
with a black square
it will be
a simple dirge
for the beautiful absence

manly regret
imprisoned
in a quadrangle

now
all space
swells like an ocean

a hurricane beats
on the black sail

the wing of a blizzard circles
over the black square

and the island sinks
beneath the salty increase

now you have
empty space
more beautiful than the object
more beautiful than the place it leaves
it is the pre-world
a white paradise
of all possibilities
you may enter there
cry out
vertical-horizontal

perpendicular lighting
strikes the naked horizon

we can stop at that
anyway you have already created a world

obey the counsels
of the inner eye

do not yield
to murmurs mutterings smackings

it is the uncreated world
crowding before the gates of your canvas

angels are offering
the rosy wadding of clouds

trees are inserting everywhere
slovenly green hair

kings are praising purple
and commanding their trumpeters
to gild
even the whale asks for a portrait

obey the counsels of the inner eye
admit no one

6

extract
from the shadow of the object
which does not exist
from polar space
from the stern reveries of the inner eye
a chair

beautiful and useless
like a cathedral in the wilderness

place on the chair
a crumpled tablecloth
add to the idea of order
the idea of adventure

let it be a confession of faith
before the vertical struggling with the horizontal

let it be
quieter than angels
prouder than kings
more substantial than a whale
let it have the face of the last things

we ask reveal o chair
the depths of the inner eye
the iris of necessity
the pupil of death

Arion

This is he—Arion—
the Grecian Caruso
concertmaster of the ancient world
expensive as a necklace
or rather as a constellation
singing
to the ocean billows and traders in silks
to the tyrants and mule herders
The crowns blacken on the tyrants' heads
and the sellers of onion cakes
for the first time err in their figures to their own disadvantage

What Arion is singing about
nobody here could say exactly
the essential thing is that he restores world harmony
the sea gently rocks the land
fire talks to water without hatred
in the shadow of one hexameter lie down
wolves and roe deer goshawks and doves
and the child goes to sleep on the lion's mane
as in a cradle
Look how the animals are smiling
People are living on white flowers
and everything is just as good
as it was in the beginning

This is he—Arion
expensive and multiple
cause of giddiness
standing in a blizzard of images
he has eight fingers like an octave
and he sings

Until from the blue in the west
unravel the luminous threads of saffron
which show that night is coming close
Arion with a friendly shake of his head
says good-by to
the mule herders and tyrants
the shopkeepers and philosophers
and in the harbor mounts the back
of a tame dolphin

—I'll be seeing you—

How handsome Arion is
—say all the girls—
when he floats out to sea
alone
with a garland of horizons on his head

Episode in a Library

A blond girl is bent over a poem. With a pencil sharp as a lancet she transfers the words to a blank page and changes them into strokes, accents, caesuras. The lament of a fallen poet now looks like a salamander eaten away by ants.

When we carried him away under machine-gun fire, I believed that his still warm body would be resurrected in the word. Now as I watch the death of the words, I know there is no limit to decay. All that will be left after us in the black earth will be scattered syllables. Accents over nothingness and dust.

The Seventh Angel

The seventh angel
is completely different
even his name is different
Shemkel

he is no Gabriel
the aureate
upholder of the throne
and baldachin

and he's no Raphael
tuner of choirs

and he's also no
Azrael
planet-driver
surveyor of infinity
perfect exponent of theoretical physics

Shemkel
is black and nervous
and has been fined many times
for illegal import of sinners

between the abyss
and the heavens
without a rest his feet go pit-a-pat

his sense of dignity is nonexistent
and they only keep him in the squad
out of consideration for the number seven
but he is not like the others

not like the hetman of the hosts
Michael
all scales and feathery plumes

nor like Azrafael
interior decorator of the universe
warden of its luxuriant vegetation
his wings shimmering like two oak trees

not even like
Dedrael
apologist and cabalist

Shemkel Shemkel
—the angels complain
why are you not perfect

the Byzantine artists
when they paint all seven
reproduce Shemkel
just like the rest

because they suppose
they might lapse into heresy
if they were to portray him
just as he is
black nervous
in his old threadbare nimbus

Rosy Ear

I thought
but I know her so well
we have been living together so many years

I know
her birdlike head
white arms
and belly

until one time
on a winter evening
she sat down beside me
and in the lamplight
falling from behind us
I saw a rosy ear

a comic petal of skin
a conch with living blood
inside it

I didn't say anything then—

it would be good to write
a poem about a rosy ear
but not so that people would say
what a subject he chose
he's trying to be eccentric

so that nobody even would smile
so that they would understand that I proclaim
a mystery

I didn't say anything then
but that night when we were in bed together
delicately I essayed
the exotic taste
of a rosy ear

Five Men

1

They take them out in the morning
to the stone courtyard
and put them against the wall

five men
two of them very young
the others middle-aged

nothing more
can be said about them

2

when the platoon
level their guns
everything suddenly appears
in the garish light
of obviousness

the yellow wall
the cold blue
the black wire on the wall
instead of a horizon

that is the moment
when the five senses rebel
they would gladly escape
like rats from a sinking ship

before the bullet reaches its destination
the eye will perceive the flight of the projectile
the ear record a steely rustle
the nostrils will be filled with biting smoke
a petal of blood will brush the palate
the touch will shrink and then slacken

now they lie on the ground
covered up to their eyes with shadow
the platoon walks away
their buttons straps
and steel helmets
are more alive
than those lying beside the wall

3

I did not learn this today
I knew it before yesterday

so why have I been writing
unimportant poems on flowers

what did the five talk of
the night before the execution

of prophetic dreams
of an escapade in a brothel
of automobile parts
of a sea voyage
of how when he had spades
he ought not to have opened
of how vodka is best
after wine you get a headache
of girls
of fruit
of life

thus one can use in poetry
names of Greek shepherds
one can attempt to catch the color of morning sky
write of love
and also
once again
in dead earnest
offer to the betrayed world
a rose

Naked Town

On the plain that town flat like an iron sheet
with mutilated hand of its cathedral a pointing claw
with pavements the color of intestines houses stripped of
    their skin
the town beneath a yellow wave of sun
a chalky wave of moon

o town what a town tell me what's the name of that town
under what star on what road

about people: they work at the slaughterhouse in an
    immense building
of raw concrete blocks around them the odor of blood
and the penitential psalm of animals Are there poets there
    (silent poets)
there are troops a big rattle of barracks on the outskirts
on Sunday beyond the bridge in prickly bushes on cold sand
on rusty grass girls receive soldiers
there are as well some places dedicated to dreams The cinema
with a white wall on which splash the shadows of the absent
little halls where alcohol is poured into glass thin and thick
there are also dogs at last hungry dogs that howl
and in that fashion indicate the borders of the town Amen

so you still ask what's the name of that town
which deserves biting anger where is that town
on the cords of what winds beneath what column of air
and who lives there people with the same skin as ours
or people with our faces or

A Halt

We halted in a town the host
ordered the table to be moved to the garden the first star
shone out and faded we were breaking bread
crickets were heard in the twilight loosestrife
a cry but a cry of a child otherwise the bustle
of insects of men a thick scent of earth
those who were sitting with their backs to the wall
saw violet now—the gallows hill
on the wall the dense ivy of executions

we were eating much
as is usual when nobody pays

JULIO CORTÁZAR

The Lines of the Hand

From a letter thrown on the table a line comes which runs across
the pine plank and descends by one of the legs. Just watch, you
see that the line continues across the parquet floor, climbs the wall
and enters a reproduction of a Boucher painting, sketches the
shoulder of a woman reclining on a divan, and finally gets out of
the room via the roof and climbs down the chain of lightning rods
to the street. Here it is difficult to follow it because of the transit
system, but by close attention you can catch it climbing the wheel
of a bus parked at the corner, which carries it as far as the docks.
It gets off there down the seam on the shiny nylon stocking of the
blondest passenger, enters the hostile territory of the customs sheds,
leaps and squirms and zigzags its way to the largest dock, and there
(but it's difficult to see, only the rats follow it to clamber aboard)
it climbs onto the ship with the engines rumbling, crosses the planks
of the first-class deck, clears the major hatch with difficulty, and in
a cabin where an unhappy man is drinking cognac and hears the
parting whistle, it climbs the trouser seam, across the knitted vest,
slips back to the elbow, and with a final push finds shelter in the
palm of the right hand, which is just beginning to close around
the butt of a revolver.

Theme for a Tapestry

The general has only eighty men, and the enemy five thousand.
In his tent the general curses and weeps. Then he writes an inspired
proclamation and homing pigeons shower copies over the enemy
camp. Two hundred foot soldiers desert to the general. There follows a skirmish which the general wins easily, and two regiments
come over to his side. Three days later, the enemy has only eighty
men and the general five thousand. Then the general writes another

proclamation and seventy-nine men join up with him. Only one enemy is left, surrounded by the army of the general who waits in silence. The night passes and the enemy has not come over to his side. The general curses and weeps in his tent. At dawn the enemy slowly unsheathes his sword and advances on the general's tent. He goes in and looks at him. The army of the general disbands. The sun rises.

The Behavior of Mirrors
on Easter Island

When you set up a mirror on the western side of Easter Island, it runs backward. When you set one up on the eastern side of the island, it runs forward. Delicate surveys may discover the point at which that mirror will run on time, but finding the point at which that mirror works correctly is no guarantee that that point will serve for any other, since mirrors are subject to the defects of the individual substances of which they are made and react the way they really and truly want to. So that Solomon Lemos, an anthropologist on fellowship from the Guggenheim Foundation, looking into the mirror to shave, saw himself dead of typhus—this was on the eastern side of the island. And at the same time a tiny mirror which he'd forgotten on the western side of Easter Island (it'd been dropped between some stones) reflected for no one Solomon Lemos in short pants on his way to school, then Solomon Lemos naked in a bathtub being enthusiastically soaped by his mummy and daddy, then Solomon Lemos going da-da-da, to the thrilled delight of his Aunt Remeditos on a cattle ranch in Trenque Lanquen county.

Instructions on How
to Wind a Watch

Death stands there in the background, but don't be afraid. Hold
the watch down with one hand, take the stem in two fingers, and
rotate it smoothly. Now another installment of time opens, trees
spread their leaves, boats run races, like a fan time continues filling
with itself, and from that burgeon the air, the breezes of earth, the
shadow of a woman, the sweet smell of bread.

What did you expect, what more do you want? Quickly strap it to
your wrist, let it tick away in freedom, imitate it greedily. Fear will
rust all the rubies, everything that could happen to it and was
forgotten is about to corrode the watch's veins, cankering the cold
blood and its tiny rubies. And death is there in the background,
we must run to arrive beforehand and understand it's already
unimportant.

Instructions on *or rather*
Examples of How to Be Afraid

In a small town in Scotland they sell books with one blank page
hidden someplace in the volume. If the reader opens to that page
and it's three o'clock in the afternoon, he dies.

In the Piazza Quirinal in Rome, there is one spot, unknown
even to the initiated after the nineteenth century, from which,
under a full moon, the statues of the Dioscuri can be seen to move,
fighting against their horses as they rear back.

At Amalfi, where the seacoast ends, there's a jetty which stretches out into the sea and night. Out beyond the last lighthouse, you can hear a dog bark.

A man is squeezing toothpaste onto his brush, all of a sudden he sees the tiny figure of a woman lying on her back, coral sort of, or a breadcrumb that's been painted.

Opening the door of the wardrobe to take out a shirt, an old almanac falls out which comes apart immediately, pages falling out and crumbling, and covers the white linen with millions of dirty paper butterflies.

There was a story about this traveling salesman whose left wrist began to hurt him, just under his wristwatch. When he removed the watch, blood spurted out. The wound showed the imprints of very tiny teeth.

The doctor finishes his examination and his conclusions are very reassuring to us. His cordial and somber voice precedes the medicines, prescriptions for which he is writing out at the moment, seated behind his desk. Every once in a while he raises his head and smiles, to cheer us up. We don't have a thing to worry about, we'll be better inside of a week. We sit at ease in our easy chair, happy, and look idly and distractedly about the room. In the shadowed area beneath the desk, suddenly we see the doctor's legs. The trousers are pulled up to just above the knees and he's wearing women's stockings.

Marvelous Pursuits

What a wonderful pursuit: cut the leg off a spider, put it in an envelope, write on it *Minister of Foreign Affairs*, add the address, run downstairs, and drop the letter into the mailbox at the corner.

What a wonderful pursuit: walk down the boulevard Arago counting the trees, and every five chestnut trees stand for a moment on one leg and wait for someone to look, then give a short, tight yell, spin like a top, arms wide, very like the *cakuy* bird who laments in the trees of northern Argentina.

What a wonderful pursuit: go into a café and ask for sugar, again for sugar, three or four times for sugar, continue with great concentration constructing a mountain of sugar, center of the table, while indignation swells along the counters and beneath the white aprons, and then spit, softly, right in the middle of the mountain, and watch the descent of the small glacier of saliva, hear the roar of broken rocks which accompanies it, arising from the contracted throats of five local customers and the boss, an honest man when he feels like it.

What a marvelous pursuit: take the bus, get off in front of the Ministry, hack your way through quickly using an official-looking envelope with heavy seals, leave the last secretary behind, and then seriously and without flinching enter the great office with mirrors, exactly at the moment that an usher in a blue uniform is delivering a letter to the Minister, watch him slit the envelope with a letter opener of historic origin, insert two fingers delicately and come out with the spider's leg and stand there looking at it, then imitate a fly's buzzing and watch how the Minister grows pale, he wants to get rid of the leg but he can't, he's trapped by the leg, turn your back and leave whistling, announce down the corridors that the Minister is resigning, and you realize that the next day enemy troops are entering the city and everything will go to hell, and it'll be a Thursday of an odd-numbered month in leap year.

Progress and Retrogression

They invented a kind of glass which let flies through. The fly would come, push a little with his head and pop, he was on the other side. Enormous happiness on the part of the fly.

All this was ruined by a Hungarian scientist when he discovered that the fly could enter but not get out, or vice versa, because he didn't know what gimmick was involved in the glass or the flexibility of its fibers, for it was very fibroid. They immediately invented a fly trap with a sugar cube inside, and many flies perished miserably. So ended any possible brotherhood with these animals, who are deserving of better luck.

FERNANDO PESSOA

Tobacco Shop

I'm nothing.
I'll always be nothing.
Not that I want to be nothing . . .
But aside from that, I contain all the dreams of the world within me.

Windows of my room,
O room of mine—one of the world's millions nobody knows
(And if they knew it, what would they know?)—
You open on the mystery of a street that people are constantly
    crossing,
A street blocked off to all thought,
A street that's real—so impossibly real, and right—so thoughtlessly
    right,
With the mystery of things lying under people and stones,
With death spreading dankness on walls and white hair on heads,
With fate driving each and every thing down oblivion street.

Today I'm bowled over, as if the truth had seized me.
Today I'm clearheaded, as if I were going to die,
Having barely enough brotherly feeling for things
To say good-by, as this house and this whole side of the street
Become a line of coaches in a long long train with a whistle
    shrieking good-by
From inside my head,
Giving a nerve-racking, bone-creaking jerk as it takes off.

Today I'm mixed up, like someone who thought something, grasped
    it, then lost it.
Today I'm torn between the allegiance I owe
The Tobacco Shop across the street—something real outside me,
And the feeling that everything's a dream—something real inside
    me.

I failed in everything.

Since I wasn't up to anything, maybe it was all really nothing.
I escaped learning anything useful
By slipping out the back window.
I went off to the country with great plans,
But found there were only trees and plants there,
And when there were people, they were just like people anywhere.
I leave my window, sit down in a chair. What should I think about?

How can I tell what I'll be—I, who don't even know what I am?
Be what I think? But I keep thinking of being so many things!
And so many people are thinking of being the same—it's impossible
    there are so many!

Genius? At this moment
A hundred thousand heads are busy thinking they're geniuses, like
    me,
And who knows if history will remember even one of them.
So from all those dreams of glory there'll be nothing but manure
    in the end.
No, I don't believe in myself.
In every asylum there are madmen sure of almost everything!
I, certain about nothing—am I more or less sure than they?
No, not even of myself . . .
In how many garrets and nongarrets of the world
Are there self-styled geniuses dreaming now?
How many aspirations, noble, high, and lucid
(Yes, really noble, high, and lucid,
And, who knows, even practicable),
Will ever see the real light of day or get a hearing?
The world is made for those born to conquer it,
Nor for those who dream of conquering it, however right they
    may be.
I've dreamt more dreams than Napoleon ever did.
I've taken to my so-called heart more humanity than Christ did.
I've secretly thought up more philosophies than Kant ever wrote
    down.
Yet I am, and perhaps will always be, the man in the garret,

Even though I don't live in one;
I'll always be *the one who wasn't born for it*;
I'll always simply be *the one who had some promise*;
I'll always be the man who stood waiting for the door to open at the
    wall that had no door,
Who sang his anthem to Infinity in a chicken coop,
Who heard the voice of God in a sealed-up well.
Believe in myself? No, I don't, nor in anything.
Let Nature pour down on my burning head
Her sun and rain, the wind that ruffles my hair,
And all the rest—let it come, if it must, or not at all,
Cardiac cases enslaved by the stars,
We've conquered the world before getting out of bed,
But we wake and the world is opaque,
We get up and the world is strange,
We go out in the street and there's the whole earth,
Plus Solar System, Milky Way—and the Big Soup.

(Go eat your chocolates, little one!
Eat your chocolates!
Look, there's no metaphysics on earth like chocolates.
Look, all the world's religions are just as edifying as making candy.
So eat, my dirty little one, eat them up!
If I could only down those chocolates as honestly as you do!
But no, I'm the thoughtful kind who peels off the silver wrapper,
    thinks, This is only tinfoil,
And throws it all on the floor, just as I've thrown my life away.)

But at least, out of my bitterness at what I'll never be,
There's the quick calligraphy of these lines,
The broken archway to Impossibility.
And at least I reserve for myself this dry-eyed contempt—
Noble, at least, in the grand gesture I make
Of casting out the dirty clothes I am, with no laundry list, into the
    drift of things,

And stay at home, shirtless.

(You who console me, who don't exist and therefore console me,
Whether Greek goddess, conceived as a statue that springs alive,
Or Roman matron, impossibly noble and nefarious,
Or Princess to troubadours, gentle and blushing,
Or eighteenth-century marchioness, so cool and *decolletée,*
Or famous courtesan back in our fathers' day,
Or modern whatever-you-are (since I can't say just what),
All that, whatever it is, if it can inspire, let it!
My heart's an empty pail.
Like someone who can call up spooks just calls up spooks,
I call myself up, and there's no answer.
I go back to the window and see the street in perfect clarity.
I see the shops, I see the pavement, I see the passing cars,
I see the dressed-up living passersby,
I see dogs too, also alive,
And all this weighs on me like a verdict of exile,
And all this is strange to me, like everything else.)

I lived, I studied, I loved, I even believed,
And now there's no beggar I don't envy simply for not being me.
In every one I see the rags, the sores, the lies,
And think: maybe you never lived, studied, loved, believed
(Because it's possible to go through the motions without doing any
    of it);
Maybe you barely existed, like the lizard whose tail's been snipped
And is just a tail, this side of the lizard, beating frantically.

What I made of myself, I shouldn't have,
And what I could have made of myself, I didn't.
The fancy dress I wore was the wrong one.
They saw me for what I wasn't; I didn't disabuse them, so I was lost.
When I decided to take off the mask,
It stuck to my face.
When I finally took it off and looked in a mirror,
I'd grown older.

I'd been drinking, and couldn't get back into the fancy dress I hadn't
    thrown away.
So I threw away the mask and slept in the cloakroom,
Like a dog that's let inside the house
Because it's harmless,
And I'm about to write this story to prove I'm sublime.

Musical essence of my useless lines,
If only I saw something in you that I'd made
And not something always fixed by the Tobacco Shop across the
    street,
Kicking at the consciousness of being alive,
Like a rug some drunkard stumbles over
Or a doormat the gypsies steal that isn't worth a dime.

But the Tobacco Shop Owner has come to the door and stands there.
I look at him, straining my half-turned neck,
Straining my half-blind soul.
He'll die and so will I.
He'll leave his signboard, I'll leave poems.
Then after a while his signboard will perish, and so will my poems.
A little later the street will die where his signboard hung,
And so will the language my poems were written in.
Then the spinning planet will die where all this happened.
In other satellites in other systems something like people
Will go on making things like poems and living under things like
    signboards,
always one thing standing against another.
always one thing as useless as another,
always the impossible thing as stupid as the real thing,
always the fundamental mystery as certain as the sleeping surface
    mystery,
always this thing or that, or neither one nor the other.

But a man has gone into the Tobacco Shop (to buy tobacco?)
And the plausible reality of it all suddenly hits me.

I'm ready to get up, full of energy, convinced, human,
And about to try to write these lines, which say the opposite.

I light a cigarette and think of writing them,
And in the cigarette I taste my liberation from all thoughts.
I follow the drifting smoke like a personal highway,
For one wakeful and knowledgeable moment enjoying
The freedom from all speculation
And the consciousness that metaphysics comes out of feeling sick.

Then I fall back in my chair
And go on smoking.
As long as fate permits I'll go on smoking.

(If I married my washwoman's daughter,
Maybe I'd be happy.)
I think of this, get up from my chair. I go to the window.

The man is leaving the Shop (putting change into his pants pocket?)
Ah, I know him: it's nonmetaphysical Stevens.
(The Tobacco Shop Owner comes back to the door.)
As if by divine instinct, Stevens turns his head my way and sees me.
He waves hello, I cry *Hello Stevens!* and the universe
Reorganizes itself for me, without hopes, without ideals, and the
    Tobacco Shop Owner smiles.

If they want me to be
a mystic, fine.
So I'm a mystic.

If they want me to be a mystic, fine. So I'm a mystic.
I'm a mystic, but only of the body.
My soul is simple; it doesn't think.

My mysticism consists in not desiring to know,
In living without thinking about it.

I don't know what Nature is; I sing it.
I live on a hilltop
In a solitary cabin.
And that's what it's all about.

Salutation to Walt Whitman

Infinite Portugal, June eleventh, nineteen hundred and fifteen . . .
A-hoy-hoy-hoy-hoy!

From here in Portugal, with all the ages in my brain,
I salute you, Walt, I salute you, my brother in the Universe,
I, with my monocle and tightly buttoned frock coat,
I am not unworthy of you, Walt, as you well know,
I am not unworthy of you, as my greeting you shows . . .
I, so like you in indolence, so easily bored,
I am with you, as you well know, and understand you and love you,
And though I never met you, born the same year you died,

I know you loved me too, you knew me and I am happy.
I know that you knew me, that you considered me and explained me,
I know that this is what I am, whether on Brooklyn Ferry ten years
   before I was born
Or strolling up *Rua do Ouro** thinking about everything that is not
   Rua do Ouro,
And just as you felt everything, so I feel everything, and so here we
   are clasping hands,
Clasping hands, Walt, clasping hands, with the universe doing a
   dance in our soul.
O singer of concrete absolutes, always modern and eternal,
Fiery concubine of the scattered world,
Great pederast brushing up against the diversity of things,
Sexualized by rocks, by trees, by people, by their trades,
Rutting on the move, with casual encounters, with mere observations,
My enthusiast for the contents of everything,
My great hero going to meet death by leaps and bounds,
Roaring, screaming, bellowing greetings to God!

Singer of cruel and tender brotherhood with everything,
Great epidermic democrat, close to all in body and soul,
Carnival of all deeds, bacchanalia of all intentions,
Twin brother of all impulses,
Jean-Jacques Rousseau of the world destined to produce machines,
Homer of all ungraspable and wavering carnality,
Shakespeare of the sensation that begins to be steam-propelled,
Milton-Shelley of the dawn of Electricity!
Incubus of all gestures,
Inner spasm of all force in objects,
Pimp of the whole Universe,
Whore of all solar systems . . .

How many times have I kissed your picture!
Wherever you are now (I don't know where it is but it is God),
You feel this, I know you feel it, and my kisses are warmer
   (among us)

---

* The main commercial and financial thoroughfare in Lisbon, equivalent in a
way to Wall Street—literally, Gold Street.

And you like it that way, dear old man, and you thank me for
them—
I know this well, something tells me, like a feeling of pleasant
warmth in my spirit,

An abstract, oblique erection at the bottom of my soul.

There was nothing of the *engageant* in you—rather the muscular,
the cyclopic,
Though in facing the Universe yours was the attitude of a woman,
For every blade of grass, every stone, every man was a Universe
for you.

Walt, my beloved old man, my great Comrade, I evoke you!
I belong to your Bacchic orgy of free sensations,
I am yours, from the tingling of my toes to' the nausea of my dreams,
I am yours, look at me—up there where you are near God, you see
me contrariwise,
From inside out . . . My body is what you divine but you see my
soul—
You see it properly, and through its eyes you glimpse my body—
Look at me: you know that I, Alvaro de Campos, engineer,
Sensationist poet,
Am not your disciple, am not your friend, am not your singer,
You know that I am You, and you are happy about it!

I could never read all your verses through . . . There's too much
feeling in them . . .
I go through your lines as through a teeming crowd brushing
past me,
And I smell the sweat, the grease, the human and mechanical
activity.
At a given moment, reading your poems, I can't tell if I'm reading
or living them,
I don't know if my actual place is in the world or in your verse,

I don't know if I'm standing here, with both feet on the ground,
Or hanging upside down in some sort of institution,

From the natural ceiling of your tumultuous inspiration,
From the middle of the ceiling of your inaccessible intensity.

Open all the doors for me!
Because I have to go in!
My password? Walt Whitman!
But I don't give any password . . .
I go in without explaining . . .
If I must, I'll knock the doors down . . .
Yes, slight and civilized though I am, I'll knock the doors down,
Because at this moment I'm not slight or civilized at all,
I'm ME, a thinking universe of flesh and bone, wanting to get in
And having to get in by force, because when I want to go in I
    am God!

Take this garbage out of my way!
Put those emotions away in drawers!
Get out of here, you politicians, literati,
You peaceful businessmen, policemen, whores, pimps,
All your kind is the letter that kills, not the spirit giving life.
The spirit giving life at this moment is ME!

Let no son of a bitch get in my way!
My path goes through Infinity before reaching its end!
It's not up to you whether I reach this end or not,
It's up to me, up to God—up to what I mean by the word *Infinite* . . .
Go on!
Press onward!
I feel the spurs, I am the very horse I mount
Because I, since I want to be consubstantial with God,
Can be everything, or I can be nothing, or anything,
Just as I please . . . It's nobody's business . . .
Raging madness! Wanting to yelp, jump,
Scream, bray, do handsprings and somersaults, my body yelling,
Wanting to grab hold of car wheels and go under them,
Get inside the whirling whip that's about to strike,
Be the bitch to all dogs and they not enough for me,
Be the steering wheel of all machines and their limitless speed,

Be the one who's crushed, abandoned, dislocated, or done for,
Come dance this fury with me, Walt, you there in that other world,
Let's swing into this rock dance, knocking at the stars,
Fall exhausted to the ground with me,
Beat the walls with me like mad,
Break down, tear yourself apart with me,
Through everything, in everything, around everything, in nothing,
In an abstract body rage that stirs up maelstroms in the soul . . .

Damn it! Get going, I said!
Even if God himself stops us, let's get going . . . it makes no
    difference . . .
Let's go on and get nowhere . . .
Infinity! Universe! End without end! What's the difference?

(Let me take off my tie, unbutton my collar.
You can't let off steam with civilization looped around your neck . . .)
All right now, we're off to a flying start!

In a great torchlight parade of all the cities of Europe,
In a great military parade of industry, trade, and leisure,
In a great race, a great incline, a great decline,
Thundering and leaping, and everything with me,
I jump up to salute you,
I yell out to salute you,
I burst loose to salute you, bounding, handstanding, yawping!

This is how I send you
My leaping verses, my bounding verses, my spasmodic verses,
My attacks-of-hysteria verses,
Verses that pull the cart of my nerves.

My crazy tumbling inspires me,
Barely able to breathe, I get to my feet exalted,
For the verses stem from my being unable to burst with life.

Open all the windows for me!
Throw open all doors!

Pull the whole house up over me!
I want to live freely, out in the open,
I want to make gestures outside my body,
To run like the rain streaming down over walls,
To be stepped on like stones down the broad streets,
To sink like heavy weights to the bottom of the sea,
And all this voluptuously, a feeling remote from me now!

I don't want the doors bolted!
I don't want the safes locked!
I want to horn in there, put my nose in, be dragged off,
I want to be somebody else's wounded member,
I want to be spilled from crates,
I want to be thrown in the ocean,
I want them to come looking for me at home with lewd intentions—
Just so I'm not always sitting here quietly,
Just so I'm not simply writing these verses!

I'm against spaces-between in the world!
I'm for the compenetrated, material contiguity of objects!
I'm for physical bodies commingling like souls,
Not just dynamically but statically too!

I want to fly and fall from way up high!
To be thrown like a hand grenade!
To be brought to a sudden stop . . . To be lifted to . . .
The highest, abstract point of me and it all!

Climax of iron and motors!
Accelerated escalator without any stairs!
Hydraulic pump tearing out my smashed-up guts!

Put me in chains, just so I can break them,
Just so I can break them with my teeth bleeding,
Bleeding away in spurts, with the masochistic joy of life!

The sailors took me prisoner,
Their hands gripped me in the dark,

For the moment I died of the pain,
My soul went on licking the floors of my private cell
While the whirling of impossibilities circled my spite.

Jump, leap, take the bit between your teeth,
Red-hot iron Pegasus of my twitching anxieties,
Wavering parking place of my motorized destiny!

He's called Walt:
Entryway to everything!
Bridge to everything!
Highway to everything!
Your omnivorous soul,
Your soul that's bird, fish, beast, man, woman,
Your soul that's two where two exist,
Your soul that's one becoming two when two are one,
Your soul that's arrow, lightning, space,
Amplex, nexus, sex and Texas, Carolina and New York,
Brooklyn Ferry in the twilight,
Brooklyn Ferry going back and forth,
Libertad! Democracy! the Twentieth Century about to dawn!
Boom! Boom! Boom! Boom! Boom!
BOOM!

You who lived it, you who saw it, you who heard it,
Subject and object, active and passive,
Here, there, everywhere you,
Circle closing off all possibilities of feeling,
Quintessence of all things that might still happen,
God-Terminus of all imaginable objects, and it is you!
You are the Hour,
You the Minute,
You the Second!
You interpolated, liberated, unfurled, and sent,
Interpolating, liberating, unfurling, sending,
You, the interpolator, liberator, unfurler, sender,
The seal on all letters,
The name on all addressed envelopes,

Goods delivered, returned, and to follow . . .
Trainful of feelings at so many soul-miles per hour,
Per hour, per minute, per second, BOOM!

Now that I'm almost dead and see everything so clearly,
I bow to you, Great Liberator.

Surely my personality has had some purpose.
Surely it meant something, since it expressed itself,
Yet looking back today, only one thing troubles me—
Not to have had your self-transcending calm,
Your star-clustered liberation from Infinite Night.

Maybe I had no mission at all on earth.

That's why I'm calling out,
For the ear-splitting privilege of greeting you,
All the ant-swarming humanity in the Universe,
All the ways of expressing all emotions,
All the consequences of all thoughts,
All the wheels, all the gears, all the pistons of the soul.

That's why I'm crying out
And why, in this homage to you from Me, they all begin to buzz
In their real and metaphysical gibberish,
In the uproar of things going on inside without nexus.

Good-by, bless you, live forever, O Great Bastard of Apollo,
Impotent and ardent lover of the nine muses and of the graces,
Cable car from Olympus to us and from us to Olympus.

I Am Tired

I am tired, that is clear,
Because, at a certain stage, people have to be tired.
Of what I am tired, I don't know:
It would not serve me at all to know
Since the tiredness stays just the same.
The wound hurts as it hurts
And not in function of the cause that produced it.
Yes, I am tired,
And ever so slightly smiling
At the tiredness being only this—
In the body a wish for sleep,
In the soul a desire for not thinking
And, to crown all, a luminous transparency
Of the retrospective understanding . . .
And the one luxury of not now having hopes?
I am intelligent: that's all.
I have seen much and understood much of what I have seen,
And there is a certain pleasure even in the tiredness this brings us,
That in the end the head does still serve for something.

OCTAVIO PAZ

Hurry

In spite of my torpor, my squinting eyes, my paunch, my appearance of having just left the cave, I never stop. I'm in a hurry. I've always been in a hurry. Night and day a bee buzzes in my brain. I jump from morning to night, sleep to waking, crowds to solitude, dawn to twilight. It's useless that each one of the four seasons offers me its opulent table; useless the canary's morning flourishes, the bed lovely as a river in summer, that adolescent and its sadness, cut off to sink into autumn. In vain, the noon sun and its crystals works, the green leaves that filter it, the rocks that deny it, the shadows that sculpt it. All of those wonders I drain in a gulp. I'm going and coming, strolling and rolling, entering and leaving. I hear music, I scratch, I think, I say, I gander. I slander, I change my clothes, I say good-by to what I was, I'll linger in what I will be. Nothing stops me. I'm in a hurry, I'm going. Where? I don't know, know nothing—except that I'm not in my place.

From when I first opened my eyes I have realized that my place isn't here where I am, but where I'm not, and never have been. Somewhere there's an empty place, and that emptiness will be filled with me and I will sit down in that hole that will be senselessly teeming with me, bubbling with me until it turns into a fountain or geyser. And then my emptiness, the emptiness of me that I am now, will fill up with itself, full of being to the brink.

I'm in a hurry to be. I run behind myself, behind my place, behind my hole. Who has reserved that place for me? What is my fate's name? Who and what is that which moves me and who and what awaits my arrival to complete itself and to complete me? I don't know, I'm in a hurry. Though I don't move from my chair, don't get out of bed. Though I turn and turn in my cage. Nailed by a name, a gesture, a tie, I move and remove. This house, these friends, these countries, these hands, this mouth, these letters that form this image that came without warning from somewhere and have stuck in my chest are not my place. Neither this nor that is my place.

All that sustains me and that I sustain sustaining my self is a screen, a wall. All that my hurry leaps. This body offers me its body, this sea pulls from its belly seven waves, seven nudes, seven smiles, seven white pleiades. I thank them and go off. Yes, the journey has been interesting, the conversation instructive, it is still early, the function has not ended, and in no way do I make the pretense of knowing the ending. I'm sorry: I'm in a hurry. I'm anxious to be free of my hurry. I'm in a hurry to wake myself and rise without saying: good-by, I'm in a hurry.

Old Poem

Escorted by obstinate memories, I take giant steps up the stairway of music. Up there on the crystal crests, the light lets fall its vestments. At the entrance, two fountains shoot up, salute me, bend their chattering plumes, and go down in a murmur that subsides. Hypocritical pomp. Inside, in rooms with portraits, someone I know plays a game of solitaire begun in 1870, someone who had forgotten me writes a letter to a friend who hasn't been born yet. Doors, smiles, quiet passages, whispers, corridors where the blood marches to the beat of mourning drums. At the bottom, in the last room, the faint light of an oil lamp. The light discusses, moralizes, debates with itself. It tells me that no one will come, to give up hope, that now it is time to put an X over everything and go to sleep. I uselessly glance over my life. My face comes off my face and falls in me like a silent rotten fruit. Not a sound, not even a sigh. And suddenly, indistinct in the light, the ancient tower, raised between yesterday and tomorrow, tall and elegant between the two abysses. I know the stairway, the worn steps, the nausea and vertigo. Here I cried, here I sang. These are the stones with which I made you, tower of burning, confused words, mountain of crumbled letters.

No. Stay if you want, to ruminate on that which was. I am setting out from the meeting with what I am, with what I now begin to be, my descendent and ancestor, my father and my son, my unlike likeness. Man begins where he died. I am going to my birth.

Natural Being

Homage to the painter Rufino Tamayo

1

The blues, spreading their robes, stretching their waterfalls, keeping vigil over their depths, transparency shaped by fire. Passionate feathers or bunches of happiness, hallucinations, hasty decisions, always skilled and chiseled, the greens gather tempers, chew well their scream before screaming, cold and dazzling from their thickness. Innumerable, gradual, implacable, the grays open to neat slashes and intrepid bugles. Adjacent to the pink, to the flame. On their shoulders rests the geometry of the furnace. Unhurt by fire, unhurt by the jungle, they are dorsal bones, they are columns, they are mercury.

In a corner the half-moon burns. It is not yet a jewel, but rather a fruit that is ripened by its own interior sun. The half-moon is radiation, womb of the mother of all, of the wife of all, pink snail that sings abandoned on a beach, night eagle. And below, next to the guitar that sings alone, the fistful of rock crystal, the hummingbird's feather, and the clock that gnaws tirelessly on the entrails, next to the objects that have just been born and those that have been on the table since the Beginning, shine the slice of watermelon, the incandescent mamey, the sliver of fire. The half-fruit is a half-moon that ripens in the sun of a woman's gaze.

Equidistant from the fruity moon and the solar fruits, suspended between the enemy worlds that pact in this smallness of chosen stuff, we glimpse our portion of totality. The Glutton shows his teeth, the Poet opens his eyes, the Woman closes hers. All is.

2

Mourning cowboys level the heights. The hooves of the savage cavalry leave a rivulet of stars. The flint lifts its stream of sharpened blackness. The planet flies to another system. The last living minute swells with pride. The howl of the furnace echoes from wall to wall, from infinity to infinity. The fool opens the bars of space and leaps toward inside himself. He disappears instantly, swallowed by himself. Beasts gnaw at the remains of the sun, astral bones, and that which is left at the Oaxaca Market. Two hawks peck a morning star in the full sky. Life flows in a straight line, guarded by two shores of eyes. At this time of war and of save-what-you-can, the lovers peer from the balcony of vertigo. They climb softly, grain of joy resting on a charred land. Their love is a magnet that attracts the world. Their kiss controls the tides and raises the floodgates of music. At the feet of their passion, reality wakes, breaks open its cocoon, spreads its wings and flies.

3

Amidst so much sleeping matter, amidst so many forms that search for their wings, their weight, their other form, the ballerina surges, lady of the red ants, tamer of music, hermit that lives in a cave of glass, beautiful woman that sleeps on the bank of a tear. She rises and dances the dance of immobility. Her navel concentrates all the rays. She is made of the glances from all the men. She is the scale that balances desire and satiety, the vessel that she gives us to sleep and wake. She is the fixed idea, the perpetual wrinkle on the forehead of man, the everlasting star. Neither dead nor living, she is the great flower that grows from the breast of the dead and the dream of the living. The great flower that every morning slowly opens its eyes and gazes without reproach at the gardener who cuts it. Her blood rises slowly through the cut stem and lifts into the air, torch that silently burns over the ruins of Mexico. Tree source, tree fountain, arch of fire, bridge of blood between the living and the dead: all is unending birth.

Letter to Two Strangers

I still do not know your name. I feel that you are so much mine that to call you by some name would be to separate myself from you, to recognize that you are distinct from the substance which makes the syllables that form my name. On the other hand, I know too well the distinction, and at what point that name interposes between us, like an impalpable and elastic wall that can never be crossed.

All this must seem confusing to you. I would like to explain how I met you, how I became aware of your presence, and why I think that you and she are and are not the same.

I don't remember the first time. Were you born with me, or was that first time so distant that it took a while to ripen in my interior, to fuse with my being? Dissolved in my self, nothing allowed me to distinguish you from the rest of me, to remind me of you, to recognize you. But the wall of silence that on certain days closed the passage to thought, the unnameable surge—the surge of emptiness—that rises from my stomach to my forehead and there installs itself like a greed that is never satisfied, a sentence that is never passed, the invisible precipice that at times opens before me, the maternal mouth of an absence—the vagina that yawns and devours me and swallows me and ejects me: to time, again to time!—, the tide and vomit that hurl me down each time when from the heights of the tower of my eyes I contemplate myself . . . everything, in sum, that which teaches me that I am nothing but an absence that throws itself forward, reveals to me—how should I say it?—your presence. You inhabit me like those impalpable grains of sand that slip into a delicate mechanism and which, while they do not impede its movement, irritate it until all the gears are corroded.

The second time: one day you ejected from my flesh upon meeting a tall blond woman, dressed in white, who waited for you smiling on a small dock. I remember the wood black and shining and the gray water playing at our feet. There was a profusion of masts, sails, boats, and chattering marine birds. Following your steps

I approached the unknown woman who took my hand without saying a word. Together we traversed the lonely coast until we came to the place of the rocks. The sea slept. There I sang and danced; there I spoke blasphemies in a language that I have forgotten. My friend at first laughed; then she began to cry. And finally fled. Nature did not ignore my challenge; while the sea pounded me with its fist, the sun descended in a straight line against me. When the stars set their claws in my charred head, I caught on fire. Later order was reestablished. The sun returned to its post and the world became immensely solitary. My friend searched for my ashes among the rocks, there where the savage birds leave their eggs.

From that day I began to pursue her. (Now I realize that in reality I was searching for you). Years later, in another country, walking quickly against a sunset that consumed the high red walls of a temple, I saw her again. I stopped her, but she did not remember me. As a pointless ruse, I succeeded in changing myself into her shadow. From then on I did not abandon her. For years and months, for atrocious minutes, I fought to wake in her the memory of our first meeting. In vain I explained to her how you had come out of me to inhabit her, our walk by the sea and my fatal imprudence. I am to her that forgotten thing that you were to me.

I spent my life in forgetting you and remembering you, in escaping you and following you. I am no more alone than, when a boy, I discovered you in the pond of that newly watered garden, no more alone than when, an adolescent, I watched you between two broken clouds, an afternoon in the ruins. But now I do not fall in my own endlessness, but in another body, in eyes that dilate and contract and devour me and ignore me, a black aperture that pulsates, living coral, greedy as a fresh wound. Body in which I lose body, body without end. If some time I stop falling, there, on the other side of the falling, perhaps life will appear to me. The true life, that which is neither night nor day, time nor untime, quiet nor motion, life seething with life, with pure liveliness. But perhaps all this is nothing but an old way of naming death. The death that was born with me and that leaves me to inhabit another body.

Marvels of the Will

At precisely three o'clock Don Pedro arrived at our table, greeted each guest, mumbled to himself some indecipherable sentences, and silently took a seat. He ordered a cup of coffee, lit a cigarette, listened to the chatter, sipped his coffee, paid the waiter, took his hat, grabbed his case, said good afternoon, and left. And so it was every day.

What did Don Pedro say upon sitting and upon rising, with serious face and hard eyes? He said:

"I hope you die."

Don Pedro said the phrase many times each day. Upon rising, upon completing his morning preparations, upon entering and leaving his house—at eight o'clock, at one, at two-thirty, at seven-forty—in the café, in the office, before and after each meal, and when lying down at night. He repeated it between his teeth or in a loud voice; alone or with others. At times only with his eyes. Always with all his soul.

No one knew to whom he addressed his words. Everyone ignored the origin of that hate. When someone wanted to dig deeper into the case, Don Pedro would turn his head with disdain, and fall silent, modest. Perhaps it was a hate without cause, a pure hate. But the sentiment nourished him, gave a seriousness to his life, majesty to his years. Dressed in black, he seemed as though he were mourning early for his victim.

One afternoon Don Pedro arrived graver than usual. He sat down heavily, and in the center of the silence that had been created before his presence, he let fall with simplicity these words:

"Now I have killed him."

Who and how? Some laughed, wanting to take the thing as a joke. Don Pedro's gaze stopped them. All of us felt uncomfortable. It was certain, the sense there of the void of death. Slowly the group dispersed. Don Pedro remained alone, more serious than ever, a little withered, like a star still burning, but tranquil, without remorse. He did not return the next day. He never returned. Did he die?

Perhaps the life-giving hate failed him. Perhaps he still lives and hates another now. I examine my actions. And I advise you to do the same, for perhaps you have felt the same obstinate, patient anger of those small myopic eyes. Have you ever thought how many—perhaps very close to you—watch you with the same eyes of Don Pedro?

Obsidian Butterfly*

They killed my brothers, my children, my uncles. On the banks of Lake Texcoco I began to weep. Whirlwinds of saltpeter rose from Peñon hill. They carried me gently and left me in the court-yard of the Cathedral. I had become so small and so gray that many mistook me for a pile of dust. Yes I, mother of the flint and of the star, I, bearer of the ray, was now but the blue feather that the bird loses in the brambles. I danced, my breasts stiff and turning, turning, turning until I became still, and then I began to sprout leaves, flowers, and fruit. In my belly the eagle throbbed. I was the mountain that you dream, the house of fire, the primordial stewpot where man is boiled and becomes man. In the night of the beheaded words my sisters and I, hand in hand, leapt and sang around the I, the only standing tower in the leveled alphabet. I still remember my songs:

> The golden throat of light
> In the thick of green sings
> Light light the headless things

They told us: the straight path never leads to winter. And now my hands tremble, the words are caught in my throat. Give me a chair and a little sun.

---

* Obsidian butterfly: *Iztapaplotl*, goddess at times confused with *Teteoinan*, our mother, and *Tonatzin*. All of these female divinities were fused in the cult that since the sixteenth century has been worshiping the Virgin of Guadalupe.

In other times, every hour was born from the vapor of my breath, danced a while on the point of my dagger and disappeared through the shining door of my hand mirror. I was the tattooed noon and the naked midnight, the little insect of jade that sings in the grass of dawn and the nightingale of clay that summons the dead. I bathed in the sun's waterfall, I bathed in myself, soaked in my own splendor. I was the flint that ripped the night clouds and opened the doors of the shower. In the Southern sky I planted gardens of fire, gardens of blood. Its coral branches still graze the foreheads of lovers. There love is the meeting of two meteors in the middle of space, and not this obstinacy of rocks rubbing each other to ignite a kiss that sizzles.

Each night is an eyelid that the thorns cannot pierce. And the day never stops, never stops to count itself, broken into copper coins. I am tired of so many beads of stone scattered in the dust. I am tired of this endless solitaire. Lucky the mother scorpion who devours her young. Lucky the spider. Lucky the snake that sheds its skin. Lucky the water that drinks itself. When will these images stop devouring me? When will I stop falling in those empty eyes?

I am alone and fallen, grain of corn loosed from the ear of time. Scatter me among the battle dead. I will be born in the eye of the captain. Rain down on me, sun me. My arid body through your body will return to a land where they sow one and harvest a hundred. Wait for me on the other side of the year: you will meet me like a lightning-flash stretched to the bank of autumn. Touch my breasts of grass. Kiss my belly, sacrificial stone. In my navel the whirlwind grows calm: I am the center fix that moves the dance. Burn, fall in me: I am the pit of living lime that cures the bones of their burden. Die in my lips. Rise from my eyes. From my body images gush: drink in these waters and remember what you forgot at birth. I am the wound that does not heal, the small solar stone: if you strike me, the world will go up in flames.

Take my necklace of tears. I wait for you from this side of time where light has inaugurated a joyous reign: the covenant of the enemy twins, the water that escapes between the fingers, and the ice, petrified like a king in his pride. There you will open my body to read the letters of your destiny.

Vrindaban

Surrounded by night
Immense forest of breathing
Vast impalpable curtains
Murmurs
      I write
I stop
    I write
       (All is and is not
And it all falls apart on the page
In silence)
      A moment ago
A car raced down the street
Among the extinguished houses
          I raced
Among my lighted thoughts
Above me the stars
         Such quiet gardens
I was a tree and spoke
Was covered with leaves and eyes
Was the rumor pushing forward
A swarm of images
(I set down now a few
Twisted strokes
        Black on white
Diminutive garden of letters
Planted in the lamp's light)
The car raced on
Through the sleeping suburb
         I raced
To follow my thoughts
        Mine and others
Reminiscences Leftovers Imaginings
Names
     The remains of sparks

The laughter of the late parties
The dance of the hours
The march of the constellations
And other commonplaces
Do I believe in man
                    Or in the stars?
I believe
          (With here a series
Of dots)
          I see

A portico of weather-eaten pillars
Statues carved by the plague
It is a double line of beggars
                              The stench
A king on his throne
                    Surrounded
By a coming and going of aromas
As if they were concubines
Pure almost corporeal undulating
From the sandalwood to the jasmine
And its phantoms
                Fever of forms
                              Fever of time
Ecstatic in its combinations
The whole universe a peacock's tail
Myriads of eyes
                Other eyes reflecting
Modulations
            Reverberations of a single eye
A solitary sun
                Hidden
Behind its cloth of transparencies
Its tide of marvels
Everything was flaming
                        Stones women water
Everything sculptured
                    From color to form

From form to fire
                    Everything was vanishing
Music of wood and metal
In the cell of the god
                              Womb of the temple
Music like spliced suns
                    Music
Like the wind and water embracing
And over the confused moans
Of matter
                The human voice
A moon in heat at midday
Complaint of the disenbodied soul
(I write without knowing the outcome
Of what I write
                    I look between the lines
My image is the lamp
                    Lit
In the middle of the night)
                              Mountebank
Ape of the absolute
                    Cowering
Pothook
          Covered with pale ashes
A sadhu looked at me and laughed
Watching me from the other shore
                              Far off, far off
Watching me like the animals like the saints
Naked   uncombed   smeared
A fixed ray a mineral glitter his eyes
I wanted to speak to him
He answered with a rumble of bowels
                              Gone   gone
Where?
          To what region of being
To what existence
                    In the open air of what worlds
In what time?

(I write
Each letter is a germ
                    The memory
Imposes its tide
And repeats its own midday)
Gone   gone
                    Saint   scoundrel   saint
In beatitudes of hunger or drugs
Perhaps he saw Krishna
                    Sparkling blue tree
Dark fountain splashing amid the drought
Perhaps in a cleft stone
He grasped the form of woman
                              Its rent
The formless dizziness
                    For this or that
He lives on the ghat where they burn the dead

The lonely streets
The houses and their shadows
All was the same and all different
The car raced on
                    I was quiet
Among my runaway thoughts
(Gone   gone
Saint   clown   saint   beggar   king   damned
It is the same
                    Always the same
                              Within the same
It is to be always within oneself
Closed up in the same
                    Closed up on oneself
Rotted idol)
                    Gone   gone
He watched me from the other shore
                              He watches me
From his interminable noon

I am in the wandering hour
The car races on among the houses
I write by the light of a lamp
The absolutes the eternities
    Their outlying districts
                Are not my theme
I am hungry for life and for death also
I know what I know and I write it
The embodiment of time
        The act
The movement in which the whole being
Is sculptured and destroyed
Consciousness and hands to grasp the hour
I am a history
      A memory inventing itself
I am never alone
I speak with you always
        You speak with me always
I move in the dark
      I plant signs

YEHUDA
AMICHAI

Out of Three or Four in a Room

Out of three or four in a room
One is always standing at the window.
Forced to see the injustice among the thorns,
The fires on the hill.

And people who left whole
Are brought home in the evening, like small change.

Out of three or four in a room
One is always standing at the window.
Hair dark above his thoughts.
Behind him, the words.
And in front of him the words, wandering, without
    luggage.
Hearts without provision, prophecies without water
And big stones put there
And staying, closed, like letters
With no addresses; and no one to receive them.

Tourist

She showed me her swaying hair
In the four winds of her coming.
I showed her some of my folding ways of life
And the trick, and the lock.
She asked after my street and my house
And I laughed loudly.
She showed me this long night
And the interior of her thirty years.
I showed her the place where I once laid *tefillin*.

I brought her chapters and verses
And sand from Eilat
And the handing of the Torah
And the manna of my death
And all the miracles that have not yet healed in me.

She showed me the stages of joy
And my childhood's double.
I revealed to her that King David is not buried in
    his tomb
And that I don't live in my life.
While I was reflecting and she was eating,
The city map lay open on the table—
Her hand on Qatamon
My hand on hers—
The cup covered the Old City,
Ash dropped on the King David Hotel,
And an ancient weeping
Allowed us to lie together.

My Mother Once Told Me

My mother once told me
Not to sleep with flowers in the room.
Since then I have not slept with flowers.
I sleep alone, without them.

There were many flowers.
But I've never had enough time.
And persons I love are already pushing themselves
Away from my life, like boats
Away from the shore.

My mother said
Not to sleep with flowers.
You won't sleep.
You won't sleep, mother of my childhood.

The bannister I clung to
When they dragged me off to school
Is long since burnt.
But my hands, clinging,
Remain
Clinging.

A Pity. We Were Such
a Good Invention

They amputated
Your thighs off my hips.
As far as I'm concerned
They are all surgeons. All of them.

They dismantled us
Each from the other.
As far as I'm concerned
They are all engineers. All of them.

A pity. We were such a good
And loving invention.
An airplane made from a man and wife.
Wings and everything.
We hovered a little above the earth.

We even flew a little.

Rain on a Battlefield

It rains on my friends' faces,
On my live friends' faces,
Those who cover their heads with a blanket.
And it rains on my dead friends' faces,
Those who are covered by nothing.

We Did It

We did it in front of the mirror
And in the light. We did it in darkness,
In water, and in the high grass.

We did it in honor of man
And in honor of beast and in honor of God.
But they didn't want to know about us,
They'd already seen our sort.

We did it with imagination and colors,
With confusion of reddish hair and brown
And with difficult gladdening
Exercises. We did it
Like wheels and holy creatures
And with chariot-feats of prophets.
We did it six wings
And six legs

But the heavens
Were hard above us
Like the earth of the summer beneath.

If I Forget Thee, Jerusalem

If I forget thee, Jerusalem,
Then let my right be forgotten,
Let my right be forgotten, and my left remember.
Let my left remember, and your right close
And your mouth open near the gate.

I shall remember Jerusalem
And forget the forest—my love will remember.
Will open her hair, will close my window,
Will forget my right,
Will forget my left,

If the west wind does not come
I'll never forgive the walls
Nor the sea, nor myself.
Should my right forget
My left shall forgive,
I shall forget all water,
I shall forget my mother.

If I forget thee, Jerusalem,
Let my blood be forgotten.
I shall touch your forehead,
Forget my own,
My voice change
For the second and last time
To the most terrible of voices—
Or silence.

JOHANNES BOBROWSKI

Childhood

Then I loved
the oriole—
the toll of bells sounded
above, sank low
through the greenwood,

when we squatted at the edge of the wood,
threaded red berries
on a grass-blade; the gray Jew
went by
with his cart.

At noon then the beasts stood
in the alders' black shadows
flicking away the flies
with angry tails.

Then the streaming rainflood
fell from the open
sky; after all that darkness
the drops tasted
like earth.

Or the lads came
along the towpath with the horses,
on the shining brown
backs they rode laughing
across the deep.

Behind the fence
hummed clouds of bees.
Later the silver rattle of fear
ran through the thorn-thicket
by the reedy lake.

It grew wild, a hedge,
darkening window and door.

Then the old woman sang in her
fragrant chamber. The lamp
hummed. The men
entered calling over their shoulders
to the dogs.

Night, long interlocked with silence—
time, slipping away, bitterer,
lasting from verse to verse:
childhood—
then I loved the oriole.

Kaunas 1941

Town,
branches over the river,
copper-colored, like branching candles.
The banks call from the deep.
Then the lame girl
walked before dusk,
her skirt of darkest red.

And I know the steps,
the slope, this house. There is no
fire. Under this roof
lives the Jewess, lives whispering

in the Jews' silence
—the faces of the daughters
a white water. Noisily
the murderers pass the gate. We walk
softly, in musty air, in the track of wolves.

At evening we looked out
over a stony valley. The hawk
swept round the broad dome.
We saw the old town, house after house
running down to the river.

Will you walk over
the hill? The gray processions
—old men and sometimes boys—
die there. They walk
up the slope ahead of the slavering wolves.

Did my eyes avoid yours
brother? Sleep struck us
at the bloody wall. So we went on
blind to everything. We looked
like gypsies at the villages
in the oak wood, the summer
snow on the roofs.

I shall walk on the stone banks
under the rainy bushes,
listen in the haze of the plains.
There were swallows upstream
and the woodpigeon called
in the green night:
My dark is already come.

North Russian Town

Pustoshka 1941

Pale
by the road to the North
falls the mountain wall. The bridge,
the old wood,
the bushy banks.

There the stream lives,
white in the pebbles, blind over the
sand. And the caw of crows
speaks your name: Wind
in the rafters, a smoke
toward the evening.

It comes,
glowing in
the cloud, it follows the winds,
it watches for the fire.

Remote fire breaks forth
in the plain,
far. Who dwell near
forests, on streams, in the wooden
luck of the villages, listen
at evening, lay
an ear to the earth.

On the Jewish Dealer A.S.

I am from Rasainen.
That is where you spend the second night
in the wood when you come from the river,
where the woods open
and yellowish sand
presses up in the meadows.

There the nights are light.
Our wives extinguish the fires
early. We breathe
long and deep with the dark
aimless sigh of the wind.

All we have,
we have from the hands of the fathers.
Their care keeps us awake.
Their starry fear
shines in the tree of our speech.
Freezing we close graves
for them. The clouds loiter
long above. Smoke.

Someone is always leaving,
does not look back, no waving
follows him. Yet the old men's
sayings at the gateposts still hold him
over the ocean. The sad music
of roads lined with birches
wakes him in the distant land.

Cathedral 1941

Which we saw
across the winter river,
across the black torrent
of the waters, Sophia, sounding
heart of benighted Novgorod.

Once before it was dark.
But a time came,
passing with gay foaming
dolphins, orchards
burnt your cheek, often
behind your fences pilgrims
halted, wet-faced,
in your cupolas' golden cry.

And your night, the moon-abyss,
deathly pale, the halcyon bird
glittered in the icy nest.

Smoke has blackened
your walls, fire broke
your doors, how shall the light
be for your window sockets.
All was done to our
life, the cry as well
as the silence, we saw
your face, white,
rising over the plains.

Then wrath sprang up
outside
in the marshes.
Wrath, a heavy seed.
How shall I call

one day
my eye still
bright.

Latvian Songs

My father the hawk.
Grandfather the wolf.
And my forefather the rapacious fish in the sea.

I, unbearded, a fool,
lurching against the fences,
my black hands strangling a lamb
in the early light. I,

who beat the animals
instead of the white
master, I follow the rattling caravans
on washed-out roads,

I pass through the glances
of the gypsy women. Then
on the Baltic shore I meet Uexküll, the master.
He walks beneath the moon.
Behind him, the darkness speaks.

The Spoor in the Sand

The pale old man
in the faded caftan.
The prayer-curl as always.
I knew your house then, Aaron.
You carry the ashes
away in your shoe.

My brother drove
you from the door. I went
after you. How the skirt
swished round your feet. I found
a spoor in the sand.

Then I saw you
sometimes in the evening
coming from the firebreak,
whispering.
With your white hands
you scattered snow like seed
over the roof of the barn.

Because your fathers' god
will brighten the years
for us, Aaron,
the spoor lies
in the dust of the street,
and I find you.
And go.
And I bear your distance,
your expectation,
on my shoulder.

CZESLAW MILOSZ

Dedication

You whom I could not save
Listen to me.
Try to understand this simple speech as I would be ashamed of
  another.
I swear, there is in me no wizardry of words.
I speak to you with silence like a cloud or a tree.

What strengthened me, for you was lethal.
You mixed up farewell to an epoch with the beginning of a new
  one,
Inspiration of hatred with lyrical beauty,
Blind force with accomplished shape.

Here is the valley of shallow Polish rivers. And an immense bridge
Going into white fog. Here is a broken city,
And the wind throws screams of gulls on your grave
When I am talking with you.

What is poetry which does not save
Nations or people?
A connivance with official lies,
A song of drunkards whose throats will be cut in a moment,
Readings for sophomore girls.
That I wanted good poetry without knowing it,
That I discovered, late, its salutary aim,
In this and only this I find salvation.

They used to pour on graves millet or poppy seeds
To feed the dead who would come disguised as birds.
I put this book here for you, who once lived
So that you should visit us no more.

Mittelbergheim

Wine sleeps in casks of Rhine oak.
I am wakened by the bell of a chapel in the vineyards
Of Mittelbergheim. I hear a small spring
Trickling into a well in the yard, a clatter
Of sabots in the street. Tobacco drying
Under the eaves, and ploughs and wooden wheels
And mountain slopes and autumn are with me.

I keep my eyes closed. Do not rush me,
You, fire, power, might, for it is too early.
I have lived through many years and, as in this half-dream,
I felt I was attaining the moving frontier
Beyond which color and sound come true
And the things of this earth are united.
Do not yet force me to open my lips.
Let me trust and believe I will attain.
Let me linger here in Mittelbergheim.

I know I should. They are with me,
Autumn and wooden wheels and tobacco hung
Under the eaves. Here and everywhere
Is my homeland, wherever I turn
And in whatever language I would hear
The song of a child, the conversation of lovers.
Happier than anyone, I am to receive
A glance, a smile, a star, silk creased
At the knee. Serene, beholding,
I am to walk on hills in the soft glow of day
Over waters, cities, roads, human customs.

Fire, power, might, you who hold me
In the palm of your hand whose furrows
Are like immense gorges combed
By southern wind. You who grant certainty

In the hour of fear, in the week of doubt,
It is too early, let the wine mature,
Let the travelers sleep in Mittelbergheim.

A Poor Christian Looks
at the Ghetto

Bees build around red liver,
Ants build around black bone.
It has begun: the tearing, the trampling on silks,
It has begun: the breaking of glass, wood, copper, nickel, silver,
foam
Of gypsum, iron sheets, violin strings, trumpets, leaves, balls,
crystals.
Poof! Phosphorescent fire from yellow walls
Engulfs animal and human hair.

Bees build around the honeycomb of lungs,
Ants build around white bone.
Torn is paper, rubber, linen, leather, flax,
Fiber, fabrics, cellulose, snakeskin, wire.
The roof and the wall collapse in flame and heat seizes the
foundations.
Now there is only the earth, sandy, trodden down,
With one leafless tree.

Slowly, boring a tunnel, a guardian mole makes his way,
With a small red lamp fastened to his forehead.
He touches buried bodies, counts them, pushes on,
He distinguishes human ashes by their luminous vapor,
The ashes of each man by a different part of the spectrum.
Bees build around a red trace.
Ants build around the place left by my body.

I am afraid, so afraid of the guardian mole.
He has swollen eyelids, like a Patriarch
Who has sat much in the light of candles
Reading the great book of the species.
What will I tell him, I, a Jew of the New Testament,
Waiting two thousand years for the second coming of Jesus?
My broken body will deliver me to his sight
And he will count me among the helpers of death:
The uncircumcised.

A Song on the End
of the World

On the day the world ends
A bee circles a clover,
A fisherman mends a glimmering net.
Happy porpoises jump in the sea,
By the rainspout young sparrows are playing
And the snake is gold-skinned as it should always be.

On the day the world ends
Women walk through the fields under their umbrellas,
A drunkard grows sleepy at the edge of a lawn,
Vegetable vendors shout in the street
And a yellow-sailed boat comes nearer the island,
The voice of a violin lasts in the air
And leads into a starry night.

And those who expected lightning and thunder
Are disappointed.
And those who expected signs and archangels' trumps
Do not believe it is happening now.
As long as the sun and the moon are above,

As long as the bumblebee visits a rose,
As long as rosy infants are born
No one believes it is happening now.

Only a white-haired old man, who would be a prophet
Yet is not a prophet, for he's much too busy,
Repeats while he binds his tomatoes:
There will be no other end of the world,
There will be no other end of the world.

To Robinson Jeffers

If you have not read the Slavic poets
so much the better. There's nothing there
for a Scotch-Irish wanderer to seek. They lived in a childhood
prolonged from age to age. For them, the sun
was a farmer's ruddy face, the moon peeped through a cloud
and the Milky Way gladdened them like a birch-lined road.
They longed for the Kingdom which is always near,
always right at hand. Then, under apple trees
angels in homespun linen will come parting the boughs
and at the white kolkhoz tablecloth
cordiality and affection will feast (falling to the ground at times).

And you are from surf-rattled skerries. From the heaths
where burying a warrior they broke his bones
so he could not haunt the living. From the sea night
which your forefathers pulled over themselves, without a word.
Above your head no face, neither the sun's nor the moon's
only the throbbing of galaxies, the immutable
violence of new beginnings, of new destruction.

All your life listening to the ocean. Black dinosaurs
wade where a purple zone of phosphorescent weeds
rises and falls on the waves as in a dream. And Agamemnon
sails the boiling deep to the steps of the palace
to have his blood gush onto marble. Till mankind passes
and the pure and stony earth is pounded by the ocean.

Thin-lipped, blue, without grace ·or hope,
before God the Terrible, body of the world.
Prayers are not heard. Basalt and granite.
Above them, a bird of prey. The only beauty.

What have I to do with you? From footpaths in the orchards,
from an untaught choir and shimmers of a monstrance,

from flower beds of rue, hills by the rivers, books
in which a zealous Lithuanian announced brotherhood, I come.
Oh, consolations of mortals, futile creeds.

And yet you did not know what I know. The earth teaches
More than does the nakedness of elements. No one with impunity
gives to himself the eyes of a god. So brave, in a void,
you offered sacrifices to demons: there were Wotan and Thor,
the screech of Erinyes in the air, the terror of dogs
when Hecate with her retinue of the dead draws near.

Better to carve suns and moons on the joints of crosses
as was done in my district. To birches and firs
give feminine names. To implore protection
against the mute and treacherous might
than to proclaim, as you did, an inhuman thing.

The Master

They say that my music is angelic.
That when the Prince listens to it
His face, hidden from sight, turns gentle.
With a beggar he would share power.
A fan of a lady-in-waiting is immobile,
Silk by its touch does not induce pleasant immodest thoughts
And under a pleat her knees, far off in a chasm, grow numb.

Everybody has heard in the cathedral my Missa Solemnis.
I changed the throats of girls from the Saint Cecilia choir
Into an instrument which raises us
Above what we are. I know how to free
Men and women from remembrances of their long lives
So that they stand in the smoke of the nave
Restored to the mornings of childhood
When a drop of dew and a shout on the mountains
Were the truth of the world.

Leaning on a cane at sunset
I may resemble a gardener
Who has planted and reared a tall tree.

I was not wasting the years of frail youthful hope.
I measure what is done. Over there a swallow
Will pass away and return, changed in its slanting flight.
Steps will be heard at the well but of other people.
The ploughs will erase a forest. The flute and the violin
Will always work as I have ordered them.

No one knows how I was paying. Ridiculous, they believe
It may be got for nothing. We are pierced by a ray.
They want a ray because this helps them to admire.
Or they accept a folktale: once, under an alder
A demon appeared to us, as black as a pond,

He drew two drops of blood with a sting of a gnat
And impressed in the wax his amethyst ring.

The celestial spheres endlessly resound.
But an instant is invincible in memory.
It comes back in the middle of the night. Who are those keeping torches,
So that what is long past occurs in full light?

Regret, to no end, in every hour
Of a long life. What beautiful work
Will redeem the heartbeats of a living creature
And what use to confess deeds that last for ever?

When old and white-haired under their laced shawls
At the entrance they dip their fingers in a basin
It seems to me she might have been one of them. The same firs
Rustle and with a shallow wave sheen the lake.

And yet I loved my destiny.
Could I move back time, I am unable to guess
Whether I would have chosen virtue. My line of fate does not tell.
Does God really want us to lose our soul
For only then He may receive a gift without blemish?

A language of angels! Before you mention Grace
Mind that you do not deceive yourself and others.
What comes from my evil—that only is true.

Elegy for N.N.

Tell me if it is too far for you.
You could have run over the small waves of the Baltic
and past the fields of Denmark, past a beech wood
could have turned toward the ocean, and there, very soon
Labrador, white at this season.
And if you, who dreamed about a lonely island,
were frightened of cities and of lights flashing along the highway
you had a path straight through the wilderness
over blue-black, melting waters, with tracks of deer and caribou
as far as the Sierra and abandoned gold mines.
The Sacramento River could have led you
between hills overgrown with prickly oaks.
Then just a eucalyptus grove, and you had found me.

True, when the manzanita is in bloom
and the bay is clear on spring mornings
I think reluctantly of the house between the lakes
and of nets drawn in beneath the Lithuanian sky.
The bath cabin where you used to leave your dress
has changed forever into an abstract crystal.
Honey-like darkness is there, near the veranda
and funny young owls, and the scent of leather.

How could one live then, I really do not know.
Styles and dresses flicker, indistinct,
not self-sufficient, tending toward a finale.
Does it matter that we long for things as they are in themselves?
The knowledge of fiery years has scorched the horses standing at the
    forge,
the little columns in the marketplace,
the wooden stairs and the wig of Mama Fliegeltaub.

We learned so much, this you know well:
how, gradually, what could not be taken away

is taken. People, countrysides.
And the heart does not die when one thinks it should,
we smile, there is tea and bread on the table.
And only remorse that we did not love
the poor ashes in Sachsenhausen
with absolute love, beyond human power.

You got used to new, wet winters,
to a villa where the blood of the German owner
was washed from the wall, and he never returned.
I too accepted but what was possible, cities and countries.
One cannot step twice into the same lake
on rotting alder leaves,
breaking a narrow sunstreak.

Guilt, yours and mine? Not a great guilt.
Secrets, yours and mine? Not great secrets.
Not when they bind the jaw with a kerchief, put a little cross
    between the fingers,
and somewhere a dog barks, and the first star flares up.

No, not because it was too far
did you not visit me that day or night.
From year to year it grows in us until it takes hold,
I understood it as you did: indifference.

NICANOR PARRA

Piano Solo

Since man's life is nothing but a bit of action at a distance,
A bit of foam shining inside a glass;
Since trees are nothing but moving trees;
Nothing but chairs and tables in perpetual motion;
Since we ourselves are nothing but beings
(As the godhead itself is nothing but God);
Now that we do not speak solely to be heard
But so that others may speak
And the echo precede the voice that produces it;
Since we do not even have the consolation of a chaos
In the garden that yawns and fills with air,
A puzzle that we must solve before our death
So that we may nonchalantly resuscitate later on
When we have led women to excess;
Since there is also a heaven in hell,
Permit me to propose a few things:

I wish to make a noise with my feet
I want my soul to find its proper body.

Journey Through Hell

On a saddle without a horse
I made a journey through hell.

In the first circle I saw
A few figures reclining
On bags of wheat.

In the second circle
Some men riding bicycles
Didn't know where to stop
Because of the flames.

In the third circle I saw
Only one human figure
It appeared to be a hermaphrodite.

A thin and twisted figure
Feeding crows.

I went on trotting and galloping
Through a space of hours
Until in a forest I came upon a cabin
Where a witch lived.

A dog tried to bite me.

In circle four
An old man with a long beard
Bald as a watermelon
Building a little boat
In a bottle.

He gave me a kind look.

In circle five
I saw some students
Playing Indian hockey
With a ball of rags.

It was savagely cold.
I had to pass the night
Keeping vigil in a graveyard
Sheltered behind a tomb
To keep from freezing.

The next day I went on
Into some hills
I saw for the first time
The skeletons of trees
Burned by the tourists.

Two circles were left.

In one I saw myself
Sitting at a black table
Eating the flesh of a bird:
My only companion
Was a kerosene stove.

In the seventh circle
I saw absolutely nothing
All I heard were strange sounds
I heard a horrible laughter
And a deep breathing
That tore open my soul.

Litany of the Little Bourgeois

If you want to get to the heaven
Of the little bourgeois, you must go
By the road of Art for Art's sake
And swallow a lot of saliva:
The apprenticeship is almost interminable.

A list of what you must learn how to do:
Tie your necktie artistically
Slip your card to the right people
Polish shoes that are already shined
Consult the Venetian mirror
(Head-on and in profile)
Toss down a shot of brandy
Tell a viola from a violin
Receive guests in your pajamas
Keep your hair from falling
And swallow a lot of saliva.

Best to have everything in your kit.
If the wife falls for somebody else
We recommend the following:
Shave with razor blades
Admire the Beauties of Nature
Crumple a sheet of paper
Have a long talk on the phone
Shoot darts with a popgun
Clean your nails with your teeth
And swallow a lot of saliva.

If he wants to shine at social gatherings
The little bourgeois
Must know how to walk on all fours
How to smile and sneeze at the same time

Waltz on the edge of the abyss
Deify the organs of sex
Undress in front of a mirror
Rape a rose with a pencil
And swallow tons of saliva.

And after all that we might well ask:
Was Jesus Christ a little bourgeois?

As we have seen, if you want to reach
The heaven of the little bourgeois,
You must be an accomplished acrobat:
To be able to get to heaven,
You must be a wonderful acrobat.

And how right the authentic artist is
To amuse himself killing bedbugs!

To escape from the vicious circle
We suggest the *acte gratuite*:
Appear and disappear
Walk in a cataleptic trance
Waltz on a pile of debris
Rock an old man in your arms
With your eyes fixed on his
Ask a dying man what time it is
Spit in the palm of your hand
Go to fires in a morning coat
Break into a funeral procession
Go beyond the female sex
Lift the top from that tomb to see
If they're growing trees in there
And cross from one sidewalk to the other
Without regard for when or why
. . . For the sake of the word alone . . .
. . . With his movie-star mustache . . .
. . . With the speed of thought . . .

The Pilgrim

Your attention, ladies and gentlemen, your attention for one
    moment:
Turn your heads for a second to this part of the republic,
Forget for one night your personal affairs,
Pleasure and pain can wait at the door:
There's a voice from this part of the republic.
Your attention, ladies and gentlemen! Your attention for one
    moment!

A soul that has been bottled up for years
In a sort of sexual and intellectual abyss,
Nourishing itself most inadequately through the nose,
Desires to be heard.

I'd like to find out some things,
I need a little light, the garden's covered with flies,
My mental state's a disaster,
I work things out in my peculiar way,
As I say these things I see a bicycle leaning against a wall,
I see a bridge
And a car disappearing between the buildings.

You comb your hair, that's true, you walk in the gardens,
Under your skins you have other skins,
You have a seventh sense
Which lets you in and out automatically.
But I'm a child calling to its mother from behind rocks,
I'm a pilgrim who makes stones jump as high as his nose,
A tree crying out to be covered with leaves.

The Tablets

I dreamed I was in a desert and because I was sick of myself
I started beating a woman.
It was devilish cold, I had to do something,
Make a fire, take some exercise,
But I had a headache, I was tired,
All I wanted to do was sleep, die.
My suit was soggy with blood
And a few hairs were stuck among my fingers
—They belonged to my poor mother—
"Why do you abuse your mother," a stone asked me,
A dusty stone, "Why do you abuse her?"
I couldn't tell where these voices came from, they gave me the
    shivers,
I looked at my nails, I bit them,
I tried to think of something but without success,
All I saw around me was a desert
And the image of that idol
My god who was watching me do these things.
Then a few birds appeared
And at the same moment, in the dark, I discovered some slabs of
    rock.
With a supreme effort I managed to make out the tablets of the law:
"We are the tablets of the law," they said,
"Why do you abuse your mother?
See these birds that have come to perch on us,
They are here to record your crimes."
But I yawned, I was bored with these warnings.
"Get rid of those birds," I said aloud.
"No," one of the stones said,
"They stand for your different sins,
They're here to watch you."
So I turned back to my lady again
And started to let her have it harder than before.

I had to do something to keep awake.
I had no choice but to act
Or I would have fallen asleep among those rocks
And those birds.
So I took a box of matches out of one of my pockets
And decided to set fire to the bust of the god.
I was dreadfully cold, I had to get warm,
But that blaze only lasted a few seconds.
Out of my mind, I looked for the tablets again
But they had disappeared.
The rocks weren't there either.
My mother had abandoned me.
I beat my brow. But
There was nothing more I could do.

The Tunnel

In my youth I lived for a time in the house of some aunts
On the heels of the death of a gentleman with whom they had been
    intimately connected
Whose ghost tormented them without pity
Making life intolerable for them.

At the beginning I ignored their telegrams
And their letters composed in the language of another day,
Larded with mythological allusions
And proper names that meant nothing to me
Some referring to sages of antiquity
Or minor medieval philosophers
Or merely to neighbors.

To give up the university just like that

And break off the joys of a life of pleasure,
To put a stop to it all
In order to placate the caprices of three hysterical old women
Riddled with every kind of personal difficulty,
This, to a person of my character, seemed
An uninspiring prospect,
A brainless idea.

Four years, just the same, I lived in The Tunnel
In the company of those frightening old ladies,
Four years of uninterrupted torture
Morning, noon, and night.
The delightful hours that I had spent under the trees
Were duly replaced by weeks of revulsion,
Months of anguish, which I did my best to disguise
For fear of attracting their curiosity.
They stretched into years of ruin and misery.
For centuries my soul was imprisoned
In a bottle of drinking water!

My spiritualist conception of the world
Left me obviously inferior to every fact I was faced with:
I saw everything through a prism
In the depths of which the images of my aunts intertwined like
    living threads
Forming a sort of impenetrable chain mail
Which hurt my eyes, making them more and more useless.

A young man of scanty means can't work things out
He lives in a bell jar called Art
Or Pleasure or Science
Trying to make contact with a world of relationships
That only exist for him and a small group of friends.

Under the influence of a sort of water vapor
That found its way through the floor of the room
Flooding the atmosphere till it blotted out everything

I spent the nights at my work table
Absorbed in practicing automatic writing.

But why rake deeper into this wretched affair?
Those old women led me on disgracefully
With their false promises, with their weird fantasies,
With their cleverly performed sufferings.
They managed to keep me enmeshed for years
Making me feel obliged to work for them, though it was never said:
Agricultural labors,
Purchase and sale of cattle,
Until one night, looking through the keyhole
I noticed that one of my aunts—
The paralytic!—
Was getting about beautifully on the tips of her toes,
And I came to, knowing I'd been bewitched.

The Viper

For years I was doomed to worship a contemptible woman
Sacrifice myself for her, endure endless humiliations and sneers,
Work night and day to feed her and clothe her,
Perform several crimes, commit several misdemeanors,
Practice petty burglary by moonlight,
Forge compromising documents,
For fear of a scornful glance from her bewitching eyes.
During brief phases of understanding we used to meet in parks
And have ourselves photographed together driving a motorboat,
Or we would go to a nightclub
And fling ourselves into an orgy of dancing
That went on until well after dawn.

For years I was under the spell of that woman.
She used to appear in my office completely naked
And perform contortions that defy the imagination,
Simply to draw my poor soul into her orbit
And above all to wring from me my last penny.
She absolutely forbade me to have anything to do with my family.
To get rid of my friends this viper made free with defamatory libels
Which she published in a newspaper she owned.
Passionate to the point of delirium, she never let up for an instant,
Commanding me to kiss her on the mouth
And to reply at once to her silly questions
Concerning, among other things, eternity and the afterlife,
Subjects which upset me terribly,
Producing buzzing in my ears, recurrent nausea, sudden fainting
    spells
Which she turned to account with that practical turn of mind that
    distinguished her,
Putting her clothes on without wasting a moment
And clearing out of my apartment, leaving me flat.

This situation dragged on for five years and more.
There were periods when we lived together in a round room
In a plush district near the cemetery, sharing the rent.
(Some nights we had to interrupt our honeymoon
To cope with the rats that streamed in through the window.)
The viper kept a meticulous account book
In which she noted every penny I borrowed from her,
She would not let me use the toothbrush I had given her myself,
And she accused me of having ruined her youth:
With her eyes flashing fire she threatened to take me to court
And make me pay part of the debt within a reasonable period
Since she needed the money to go on with her studies.
Then I had to take to the street and live on public charity,
Sleeping on park benches
Where the police found me time and again, dying,
Among the first leaves of autumn.
Fortunately that state of affairs went no further,

For one time—and again I was in a park,
Posing for a photographer—
A pair of delicious feminine hands suddenly covered my eyes
While a voice that I loved asked me: Who am I.
You are my love, I answered serenely.
My angel! she said nervously.
Let me sit on your knees once again!
It was then that I was able to ponder the fact that she was now
 wearing brief tights.
It was a memorable meeting, though full of discordant notes.
I have bought a plot of land not far from the slaughterhouse, she
 exclaimed.
I plan to build a sort of pyramid there
Where we can spend the rest of our days.
I have finished my studies, I have been admitted to the bar,
I have a tidy bit of capital at my disposal,
Let's go into some lucrative business, we two, my love, she added,
Let's build our nest far from the world.
Enough of your foolishness, I answered, I have no confidence in
 your plans.
Bear in mind that my real wife
Can at any moment leave both of us in the most frightful poverty.
My children are grown up, time has elapsed,
I feel utterly exhausted, let me have a minute's rest,
Get me a little water, woman,
Get me something to eat from somewhere,
I'm starving,
I can't work for you any more,
It's all over between us.

Madrigal

I'm going to make a million some night
With a gadget for fixing images
In a concave mirror. Or a convex one.

I think my work will be a complete success
When I have perfected the coffin with a double bottom
So the corpse can take a look into the other world.

I have busted my gut enough
In this absurd horse race
Where the jockeys are thrown from their saddles
And land among the spectators.

It's fair, then, to try to believe something
That will let me live an easy life
Or at least die.

I know my legs are trembling
I dream my teeth are falling out
And that I come late to a funeral.

I Take Back
Everything I've Said

Before I go
I'm supposed to get a last wish:
Generous reader
            burn this book
It's not at all what I wanted to say
In spite of the fact that it was written with blood
It's not what I wanted to say.

No lot could be sadder than mine
I was defeated by my own shadow:
The words take vengeance against me.

Forgive me, reader, good reader
If I cannot leave you
With a faithful gesture. I leave you
With a forced and sad smile.

Maybe that's all I am
But listen to my last word:
I take back everything I've said.
With the greatest bitterness in the world
I take back everything I've said.

CARLOS DRUMMOND DE ANDRADE

Souvenir of the Ancient World

Clara strolled in the garden with the children.
The sky was green over the grass,
the water was golden under the bridges,
other elements were blue and rose and orange,
a policeman smiled, bicycles passed,
a girl stepped onto the lawn to catch a bird,
the whole world—Germany, China—all was quiet around Clara.

The children looked at the sky: it was not forbidden.
Mouth, nose, eyes were open. There was no danger.
What Clara feared were the flu, the heat, the insects.
Clara feared missing the eleven o'clock trolley,
waiting for letters slow to arrive,
not always being able to wear a new dress. But she strolled in the
    garden, in the morning!
They had gardens, they had mornings in those days!

The Elephant

I make an elephant
from the little
I have. Wood
from old furniture
holds him up, and I fill him
with cotton, silk,
and sweetness.
Glue keeps his heavy
ears in place.
His rolled-up trunk
is the happiest part
of his architecture.
And his tusks are made
of that rare material
I cannot fake.
A white fortune
rolling around
in the dust of the circus
without being stolen or lost!
And finally there are
the eyes where the most
fluid and permanent
part of the elephant
stays, free of dishonesty.

Here's my poor elephant
ready to leave
to find friends
in a tired world
that no longer believes
in animals and doesn't
trust in things.
Here he is: an imposing

and fragile hulk,
who shakes his head
and moves slowly,
his hide stitched
with cloth flowers
and clouds, allusions
to a more poetic world
where love reassembles
the natural forms.

My elephant goes
down a crowded street,
but nobody looks
not even to laugh
at his tail that threatens
to leave him.
He is all grace, except
his legs don't help
and his swollen belly
will collapse
at the slightest touch.
He expresses
with elegance
his minimal life
and no one in town
is willing to take
to himself
from that tender body
the fugitive image,
the clumsy walk.

Easily moved,
he yearns for
sad situations,
unhappy people,
moonlit encounters
in the deepest ocean,

under the roots of trees,
in the bosom of shells;
he yearns for lights
that do not blind
yet shine into
the shade surrounding
the thickest trunks;
he walks the battlefield,
without crushing plants,
searching for places,
secrets, stories
untold in any book,
whose style only the wind,
the leaves, the ant
recognize, but men
ignore since they dare
show themselves only
under a veiled peace
and to closed eyes.

And now late at night
my elephant returns,
but returns tired out,
his shaky legs
break down in the dust.
He didn't find
what he wanted,
what he wanted,
I and my elephant,
in whom I love
to disguise myself.
Tired of searching,
his huge machinery
collapses like paper
The paste gives way
and all his contents,
forgiveness, sweetness,
feathers, cotton,

burst out on the rug,
like a myth torn apart.
Tomorrow I begin again.

Quadrille

John loved Teresa who loved Raymond
who loved Mary who loved Jack who loved Lily
who didn't love anybody.
John went to the United States, Teresa to a convent,
Raymond died in an accident, Mary became an old maid,
Jack committed suicide and Lily married J. Pinto Fernandez
who didn't figure into the story.

The Dead in Frock Coats

In the corner of the living room was an album of unbearable photos,
many meters high and infinite minutes old,
over which everyone leaned
making fun of the dead in frock coats.

Then a worm began to chew the indifferent coats,
the pages, the inscriptions, and even the dust on the pictures.
The only thing it did not chew was the everlasting sob of life that
    broke
and broke from those pages.

Wandering

Urn
that my aunt carried through Brazil
with the ashes of her love turned pure
mixed with the black dress the white apron the dark lips
crystal urn sand urn eighteenth-century urn
urn wet with big tears and rain from the road
crude urn carved by Andrade passion without peace or letup
twenty years a traveler
urn urn urn
like a scream in the skin of night the cry of an animal
yet blue and painted with little flowers
urn in which I sleep curled up
myself an urn of my own private ashes

Don't Kill Yourself

Carlos, calm down, love
is what you are seeing:
a kiss today, tomorrow no kiss,
the day after tomorrow is Sunday
and nobody knows what will happen
on Monday.

It's useless to resist
or to commit suicide.
Don't kill yourself. Don't kill yourself.
Save all of yourself for the wedding
though nobody knows when or if
it will ever come.

Carlos, earthy Carlos, love
spent the night with you
and your deepest self
is raising a terrible racket,
prayers,
victrolas,
saints in procession,
ads for the best soap,
a racket for which nobody knows
the why or wherefor.

Meanwhile, you walk
upright, unhappy.
You are the palm tree, you are the shout
that nobody heard in the theater
and all the lights went out.
Love in darkness, no, in daylight,
is always sad, Carlos, my boy,
don't tell anyone,
nobody knows or will know.

The Dirty Hand

My hand is dirty.
I must cut it off.
To wash it is pointless.
The water is putrid.
The soap is bad.
It won't lather.
The hand is dirty.
It's been dirty for years.

I used to keep it
out of sight,
in my pants' pocket.
No one suspected a thing.
People came up to me,
wanting to shake hands.
I would refuse
and the hidden hand
would leave its imprint
on my thigh.
And I saw
it was the same
if I used it or not.
Disgust was the same.

How many nights
in the depths of the house
I washed that hand,
scrubbed it, polished it,
dreamed it would turn
to diamond or crystal
or even, at last,
into a plain white hand,

the clean hand of a man,
that you could shake,
or kiss, or hold
in one of those moments
when two people confess
without saying a word . . .
Only to have
the incurable hand
open its dirty fingers

And the dirt was vile.
It was not mud or soot
or the caked filth
of an old scab
or the sweat
of a laborer's shirt.
It was a sad dirt
made of sickness
and human anguish.
It was not black;
black is pure.
It was dull,
a dull grayish dirt.

It is impossible
to live with this
gross hand that lies
on the table.
Quick! Cut it off!
Chop it to pieces
and throw it
into the ocean.
With time, with hope
and its intricate workings
another hand will come,
pure, transparent as glass,
and fasten itself to my arm.

Your Shoulders
Hold Up the World

A time comes when you no longer can say: my God.
A time of total cleaning up.
A time when you no longer can say: my love.
Because love proved useless.
And the eyes don't cry.
And the hands do only rough work.
And the heart is dry.

Women knock at your door in vain, you won't open.
You remain alone, the light turned off,
and your enormous eyes shine in the dark.
It is obvious you no longer know how to suffer.
And you want nothing from your friends.

Who cares if old age comes, what is old age?
Your shoulders are holding up the world
and its lighter than a child's hand.
Wars, famine, family fights inside buildings
prove only that life goes on
and nobody will ever be free.
Some (the delicate ones) judging the spectacle cruel
will prefer to die.
A time comes when death doesn't help.
A time comes when life is an order.
Just life, with no escapes.

PAUL
CELAN

Corona

Autumn eats its leaf out of my hand: we are friends.
From the nuts we shell time and we teach it to walk:
then time returns to the shell.

In the mirror it's Sunday,
in dream there is room for sleeping,
our mouths speak the truth.

My eye moves down to the sex of my loved one:
we look at each other,
we exchange dark words,
we love each other like poppy and recollection,
we sleep like wine in the conches,
like the sea in the moon's blood ray.

We stand by the window embracing, and people look up from the
    street:
it is time they knew!
It is time the stone made an effort to flower,
time unrest had a beating heart.
It is time it were time.

It is time.

Aspen Tree...

Aspen tree, your leaves glance white into the dark.
My mother's hair was never white.

Dandelion, so green is the Ukraine.
My yellow-haired mother did not come home.

Rain cloud, above the well do you hover?
My quiet mother weeps for everyone.

Round star, you wind the golden loop.
My mother's heart was ripped by lead.

Oaken door, who lifted you off your hinges?
My gentle mother cannot return.

Shibboleth

Together with my stones
grown big with weeping
behind the bars,

they dragged me out into
the middle of the market,
that place
where the flag unfurls to which
I swore no kind of allegiance.

Flute,
double flute of night:
remember the dark

twin redness
of Vienna and Madrid.

Set your flag at half-mast,
memory.
At half-mast
today and forever.

Heart:
here too reveal what you are,
here, in the midst of the market.
Call the shibboleth, call it out
into your alien homeland:
February. *No pasaran.*

Unicorn:
you know about the stones,
you know about the water;
come,   .
I shall lead you away
to the voices
of Estremadura.

Psalm

No one molds us again out of earth and clay,
no one conjures our dust.
No one.

Praised be your name, no one.
For your sake
we shall flower.
Toward
you.

A nothing
we were, are, shall
remain, flowering;
the nothing-, the
no one's rose.

With our pistil soul-bright
with our stamen heaven-ravaged
our corolla red
with the crimson word which we sang
over, o over
the thorn.

Chanson of a Lady in the Shade

When the silent one comes and beheads the tulips:
Who wins?
    Who loses?
        Who walks to the window?
Who's the first to speak her name?

He is one who wears my hair.
He wears it much as one wears the dead on one's hands.
He wears it much as the sky wore my hair that year
    when I loved.
He wears it like that out of vanity.

That one wins.
    Doesn't lose.
        Doesn't walk to the window.
He does not speak her name.

He is one who has my eyes.
He's had them since gates have shut.
He wears them like rings on his fingers.
He wears them like shards of sapphire and lust;
Since the autumn he has been my brother;
He's counting the days and the nights.

That one wins.
    Doesn't lose.
        Doesn't walk to the window.
He's the last to speak her name.

He's one who has what I said.
He carries it under his arm like a bundle.
He carries it as the clock carries its worst hour.
From threshold to threshold he carries it, never throws
    it away.

That one doesn't win.
　　He loses.
　　　　He walks to the window.
He's the first to speak her name.

With tulips that one's beheaded.

Fugue of Death

Black milk of daybreak we drink it at nightfall
we drink it at noon in the morning we drink it at night
drink it and drink it
we are digging a grave in the sky it is ample to lie there
A man in the house he plays with the serpents he writes
he writes when the night falls to Germany your golden hair
   Margarete
he writes it and walks from the house the stars glitter he whistles
   his dogs up
he whistles his Jews out and orders a grave to be dug in the earth
he commands us strike up for the dance

Black milk of daybreak we drink you at night
we drink in the mornings at noon we drink you at nightfall
drink you and drink you
A man in the house he plays with the serpents he writes
he writes when the night falls to Germany your golden hair
   Margarete
Your ashen hair Shulamith we are digging a grave in the sky it is
   ample to lie there

He shouts stab deeper in earth you there and you others you sing
   and you play
he grabs at the iron in his belt and swings it and blue are his eyes
stab deeper your spades you there and you others play on for the
   dancing

Black milk of daybreak we drink you at nightfall
we drink you at noon in the mornings we drink you at nightfall
drink you and drink you
a man in the house your golden hair Margarete
your ashen hair Shulamith he plays with the serpents

He shouts play sweeter death's music death comes as a master from
  Germany
he shouts stroke darker the strings and as smoke you shall climb to
  the sky
then you'll have a grave in the clouds it is ample to lie there

Black milk of daybreak we drink you at night
we drink you at noon death comes as a master from Germany
we drink you at nightfall and morning we drink you and drink you
a master from Germany death comes with eyes that are blue
with a bullet of lead he will hit in the mark he will hit you
a man in the house your golden hair Margarete
he hunts us down with his dogs in the sky he gives us a grave
he plays with the serpents and dreams death comes as a master from
  Germany

your golden hair Margarete
your ashen hair Shulamith.

Your Hand Full of Hours

Your hand full of hours, you came to me—and I said:
Your hair is not brown.
So you lifted it lightly on to the scales of grief; it weighed more
than I . . .

On ships they come to you and make it their cargo, then put it on
sale in the markets of lust—
You smile at me from the depth, I weep at you from the scale that
stays light.
I weep: Your hair is not brown, they offer brine from the sea and
you give them curls . . .
You whisper: They're filling the world with me now, in your heart
I'm a hollow way still!
You say: Lay the leafage of years beside you—it's time you came
closer and kissed me!

The leafage of years is brown, your hair is not brown.

MIROSLAV HOLUB

The Fly

She sat on a willow trunk
watching
part of the battle of Crécy,
the shouts,
the gasps,
the groans,
the tramping and the tumbling.

During the fourteenth charge
of the French cavalry
she mated
with a brown-eyed male fly
from Vadincourt.

She rubbed her legs together
as she sat on a disemboweled horse
meditating
on the immortality of flies.

With relief she alighted
on the blue tongue
of the Duke of Clervaux.

When silence settled
and only the whisper of decay
softly circled the bodies

and only
a few arms and legs
still twitched jerkily under the trees,

she began to lay her eggs
on the single eye

of Johann Uhr,
the Royal Armourer.

And thus it was
that she was eaten by a swift
fleeing
from the fires of Estrées.

Cinderella

Cinderella is sorting the peas:
good ones, bad ones,
yes and no, yes and no.
And she doesn't cheat. She doesn't deceive.

Somewhere there is laughter late.
They bring the horses for someone
who is to ride in state.

The shoe is not really small,
you only have to cut off your toes:
that is the truth and it goes for all.

Cinderella is sorting the peas:
good ones, bad ones,
yes and no, yes and no.
And she doesn't cheat. She doesn't deceive.

The coaches with jingle-bells have arrived,
at the ball they all bow
to the self-appointed bride.

No blood flows, only red birds

have come from far away,
their feathers torn on the way.

Cinderella is sorting the peas,
good ones, bad ones,
yes and no, yes and no.

There are no nuts, no prince,
no doves, no mummy,
and there is only one hope:
Cinderella is sorting the peas.

Quietly, as when one fastens the rafters,
pieces together the clockwork,
or simply mixes bread.

And may be it's lighter than air,
may be only a song in the mind,
may be only a blown feather.

Cinderella is sorting the peas:
bad ones, good ones,
yes and no, yes and no.

Cinderella knows. She knows the story,
knows that one day, and without glory,
the peas will be sorted. Even though . . .

Man Cursing the Sea

Someone
just climbed to the top of the cliff
and started cursing the sea:

Stupid water, stupid pregnant water,
slimy copy of the sky,
hesitant hoverer between the sun and the moon,
pettifogging reckoner of shells,
fluid, loud-mouthed bull,
fertilizing the rocks with his blood,
suicidal sword
splintering itself on any promontory,
hydra, fragmenting the night,
breathing salty clouds of silence,
spreading jelly-like wings
in vain, in vain,
gorgon, devouring its own body,

water, you absurd flat skull of water—

Thus for a while he cursed the sea,
which licked his footprints in the sand
like a wounded dog.

And then he came down
and stroked
the small immense stormy mirror of the sea.

There you are, water, he said,
and went his way.

Žito the Magician

To amuse His Royal Majesty he will change water into wine.
Frogs into footmen. Beetles into bailiffs. And make a Minister
out of a rat. He bows, and daisies grow from his fingertips.
And a talking bird sits on his shoulder.

There.

Think up something else, demands His Royal Majesty.
Think up a black star. So he thinks up a black star.
Think up dry water. So he thinks up dry water.
Think up a river bound with straw-bands. So he does.

There.

Then along comes a student and asks: Think up sine alpha
greater than one.

And Žito grows pale and sad: Terribly sorry. Sine is
between plus one and minus one. Nothing you can do about
that.
And he leaves the great royal empire, quietly weaves his way
through the throng of courtiers, to his home
in a nutshell.

Suffering

Ugly creatures, ugly grunting creatures,
Completely concealed under the point of the needle,
    behind the curve of the Research Task Graph,
Disgusting creatures with foam at the mouth,
    with bristles on their bottoms,
One after the other
They close their pink mouths
They open their pink mouths
They grow pale
Flutter their legs
    as if they were running a very
    long distance,

They close ugly blue eyes,
They open ugly blue eyes
    and
    they're
    dead.

But I ask no questions,
no one asks any questions.

And after their death we let the ugly creatures
    run in pieces along the white expanse
    of the paper electrophore
We let them graze in the greenish-blue pool
    of the chromatogram
And in pieces we drive them for a dip
    in alcohol
    and xylol
And the immense eye of the ugly animal god
    watches their every move

through the tube of the microscope

And the bits of animals are satisfied
like flowers in a flowerpot
   like kittens at the bottom of a pond
   like cells before conception.
But I ask no questions,
   no one asks any questions,
Naturally no one asks
Whether these creatures wouldn't have preferred
   to live all in one piece,
   their disgusting life
   in bogs
   and canals,
Whether they wouldn't have preferred to eat
   one another alive,
Whether they wouldn't have preferred to make love
in between horror and hunger,
Whether they wouldn't have preferred to use
   all their eyes and pores to perceive
   their muddy stinking little world
Incredibly terrified,
Incredibly happy
In the way of matter which can do no more.

But I ask no questions,
   no one asks any questions,
Because it's all quite useless,
Experiments succeed and experiments fail,
Like everything else in this world,
   in which the truth advances
   like some splendid silver bulldozer
   in the tumbling darkness,

Like everything else in this world,
   in which I met a lonely girl
   inside a shop selling bridal veils,
In which I met a general covered
   with oak leaves,

In which I met ambulance men who could find no
wounded,
In which I met a man who had lost
his name,
In which I met a glorious and famous, bronze,
incredibly terrified rat,
In which I met people who wanted to lay down
their lives and people who wanted to lay down
their heads in sorrow,
In which, come to think of it, I keep meeting my
own self at every step.

YANNIS
RITSOS

The Poet's Place

The black, carved writing desk, the two silver candlesticks,
his red pipe. He sits, unseen almost, in the armchair,
keeping the window always at his back. From behind his
enormous, cautious spectacles he observes his guest
bathed in light; himself hidden among his words,
in history, in his personal masks, distanced, invulnerable
snaring people's attention with the subtle reflections
of a sapphire which he wears on his finger, and always eagerly
savoring their expressions, at the moment when the simple boys
moisten their lips with their tongues in amazement. And he,
crafty, voracious, sensual, the supreme innocent,
between Yes and No, desire and repentance,
completely poised, like a balance in the hand of God,
while the light from the window behind his head
sets on him a crown of forgiveness and sanctity.
"If poetry is not absolution"—he whispered to himself—
"then we can expect pity from nowhere else."

Putting Out the Lamp

The time of great fatigue comes. The morning dazzling,
treacherous—it signals the end of yet another of his nights, outdoes
the bright remorse of the mirror, resentfully chiseling
ravines about his lips and eyes. Now,
the mildness of the lamp and the closed curtains are of no use.
Inflexible awareness of the end above the sheets which cool
the warm breath of the summer night, and only a few ringlets
   remain
fallen from the curls of a young head—a severed chain—
this same chain, who forged it? No,
neither memory nor poetry is of any use. Nevertheless,
in the last moment before he sleeps, bending over the glass of the
   lamp
to blow out its flame, to extinguish even that once more, he realizes
that he is breathing down into the glass ear of eternity
a deathless word, completely his own, his own breath, the sigh of
   creation.
Wonderful how the lamp's smoke perfumes his room in the dawn.

Final Hour

A perfume remained in his room, perhaps only
from recollection, and it might have been from the window
half open to the spring evening. He picked out
the things which he would take with him. He covered
the large mirror with a sheet. And still
in his fingers that sensation of shapely bodies
and the sensation, the solitary sensation, of his pen—no contrast:
the ultimate union of poetry. He had not wanted
to deceive anyone. The end was near. He asked
once again: "Gratitude, perhaps, or the desire
for gratitude?" His ancient slippers had wandered
under his bed. He did not want
to cover them—(O, certainly, some other time). Only,
when he had put the key in his waistcoat pocket,
he sat on his case, right in the center of the room,
totally alone, and began to weep, recognizing,
for the first time with such certainty, his innocence.

Dusk

You know that moment in the summer dusk
in the closed room; the faintest rosy gleam
across the planking of the ceiling; and the poem
half finished on the table—two verses in all,
an unredeemed promise of a delightful journey,
of a certain freedom, a certain independence,
a certain (relative, of course) immortality.

Outside on the road, already the appeal of night,
the weightless shadows of gods, men, bicycles,
when work has ended on the building sites and the young laborers
with their tools, their wet, luxuriant hair,
with small flecks of lime on their worn clothes
vanish into the evening mists and become divine.

Eight decisive strokes on the grandfather clock above the stairs,
the whole length of the corridor—inexorable strokes
of an imperious hammer hidden behind the shaded
glass; and simultaneously the age-old clatter
of those keys about which he could never with certainty
discover whether they were unlocking or locking up.

Alone with His Work

All night he galloped alone, in wild excitement, pitilessly spurring
his horse's flanks. They were waiting for him, he said, undoubtedly,
there was great urgency. When he arrived at dawn
no one was waiting, there was no one. He looked all around.
Desolate houses, bolted. They were asleep.
He heard beside him his horse panting—
foam on his mouth, sores on his ribs, his back flayed.
He hugged his horse's neck and began to weep.
The horse's eyes, large, dark, near to death,
were two towers standing alone, far away, in a land where it was
   raining.

Miniature

The woman stood up in front of the table. Her sad hands
begin to cut thin slices of lemon for tea
like yellow wheels for a very small carriage
made for a child's fairy tale. The young officer opposite:
sunk in the old arm chair. He doesn't look at her.
He lights up his cigarette. His hand holding the match trembles,
throwing light on his tender chin and the teacup's handle. The clock
holds its heartbeat for a moment. Something has been postponed.
The moment has gone. It's too late now. Let's drink our tea.
Is it possible, then, for death to come in that kind of carriage?
To pass by and leave? And only this carriage to remain
with its little yellow wheels of lemon on a side street with unlit
   lamps,
and then a small song, a little mist, and then nothing?

Beauty

Naked, she took the red handkerchief
and covered her eyes so as not to be seen;
in case fear would force them to look.
Silent and arrogant—maybe even afraid,
within the darkness of her concealed eyes,
she may have even touched or even mixed the light.
Then she did not wake.

Under the straw chair of the garden, her shoes remained
with the bare form of her feet. On the tree branch,
her white dress streamed unfastening all her nudity.

She had hoped for this after death. The light of the garden
fluttered—I don't know how—like mocking, like applause.

Insignificant Needs

The houses jammed one on top of the other,
or face to face, without exchanging glances. The elbows
of the chimneys shove each other in the night. The bakery's light
is a sigh that allows a small passage on the street.
A cat looks behind her. Vanishes. A man
entered his room. On his blanket,
over his iron bed, he found reclining
the crowded desolation of the city. As he was undressing,
he recalled that he hadn't noticed if there was a moon.
The bulks of the houses were shuffling in his memory
like cards in a closed, secretive gambling room
where all the players had lost. And he needed to imagine
that someone must love him, within these numberless houses,
so that he could sleep, so that he could wake up.
But, yes, of course, there was a moon—he remembered
the illumination of a ditch with soap water.

VASKO POPA

The Stargazer's Legacy

His words were left after him
More beautiful than the world
No one dares to look at them long

They wait around time's turnings
Greater than men
Who can pronounce them

They lie on the mute earth
Heavier than bones of life
Death wasn't able
To carry off as dowry

No one can lift them
No one can drop them

The falling stars tuck their heads
In the shadows of his words

Proud Error

Once upon a time there was an error
So ridiculous so minute
No one could have paid attention to it

It couldn't stand
To see or hear itself

It made up all sorts of nonsense
Just to prove
That it really didn't exist

It imagined a space
To fit all its proofs in
And time to guard its proofs
And the world to witness them

All that it imagined
Was not so ridiculous
Or so minute
But was of course in error

Was anything else possible

Forgetful Number

Once upon a time there was a number
Pure and round like the sun
But lonely very lonely

It started to calculate by itself

It divided multiplied
Subtracted and added itself
But remained always alone

It stopped calculating
And shut itself away
In its rounded sunlit innocence

The glowing tracks of its calculations
Stayed outside

They began to hunt each other in the dark
To divide themselves without multiplying
To subtract themselves while adding

That's the way it goes in the dark

No one was left to plead to it
To call back its tracks
And rub them out

Echo Turned to Stone

Once upon a time there were so many echoes
They were slaves of one voice
Built him arches

The arches tumbled down
They'd built them crooked
The dust buried them

They gave up the dangerous labor
Turned to stone from hunger

Turned to stone they flew
To find to rip to bits the lips
From which the voice came

They flew no one knows how long
Blind fools they didn't notice
That they flew along the edge of the lips
They were seeking

Prudent Triangle

Once upon a time there was a triangle
It had three sides
The fourth it kept hidden
In its burning center

By day it climbed its three peaks
And admired its center
At night it rested
In one of its three angles

Each dawn it watched its three sides
Turn into three fiery wheels
And vanish in the blue of never return

It took its fourth side
Embraced it and broke it three times
To hide it again in its old place

And again it had only three sides

And again it climbed each day
To its three peaks
And admired its center
While at night it rested
In one of its angles

The Tale About a Tale

Once upon a time there was a tale

It came to the end
Before its beginning
And began
After its end

Its heroes entered it
After their death
And left it
Before their birth

Its heroes spoke
Of an earth of a heaven
They spoke a lot

Only they didn't say
What even they didn't know
That they are heroes in a tale

In a tale coming to the end
Before its beginning
And beginning
After its end

The Yawn of Yawns

Once upon a time there was a yawn
Neither under the palate nor under the hat
Neither in the mouth nor in everything

It was bigger than all
Bigger than its own bigness

From time to time
Its dense night its hopeless night
Would glitter hopelessly here and there
You'd think there were stars

Once upon a time there was a yawn
Boring as any yawn
And it still seems to go on and on

The Little Box

The little box gets her first teeth
And her little length
Little width little emptiness
And all the rest she has

The little box continues growing
The cupboard that she was inside
Is now inside her

And she grows bigger bigger bigger
Now the room is inside her
And the house and the city and the earth
And the world she was in before

The little box remembers her childhood
And by a great great longing
She becomes a little box again

Now in the little box
You have the whole world in miniature
You can easily put it in a pocket
Easily steal it easily lose it

Take care of the little box

The Tenants of the Little Box

Throw into the little box
A stone
You'll take out a bird

Throw in your shadow
You'll take out the shirt of happiness

Throw in your father's root
You'll take out the axle of the universe

The little box works for you

Throw into the little box
A mouse
You'll take out a shaking hill

Throw in your mother pearl
You'll take out the chalice of eternal life

Throw in your head
You'll take out two

The little box works for you

The Craftsmen of
the Little Box

Don't open the little box
Heaven's hat will fall out of her

Don't close her for any reason
She'll bite the trouser leg of eternity

Don't drop her on the earth
The sun's eggs will break inside her

Don't throw her in the air
Earth's bones will break inside her

Don't hold her in your hands
The dough of the stars will go sour inside her

What are you doing for God's sake
Don't let her get out of your sight

The Victims of the Little Box

Not even in a dream
Should you have anything to do
With the little box

If you saw her full of stars once
You'd wake up
Without heart or soul in your chest

If you slid your tongue
Into her keyhole once
You'd wake up with a hole in your forehead

If you ground her to bits once
Between your teeth
You'd get up with a square head

If you ever saw her empty
You'd wake up
With a belly full of mice and nails

If in a dream you had anything to do
With the little box
You'd be better off never waking up

The Enemies of the Little Box

Don't bow down before the little box
Which supposedly contains everything
Your star and all other stars

Empty yourself
In her emptiness

Take two nails out of her
And give them to the owners
To eat

Make a hole in her middle
And stick on your clapper

Fill her with blueprints
And the skin of her craftsmen
And trample on her with both feet

Tie her to the cat's tail
And chase the cat

Don't bow down to the little box
If you do
You'll never straighten yourself out again

The Judges of the Little Box

To Karl Max Ostojić

Why do you stare at the little box
That in her emptiness
Holds the whole world

If the little box holds
The world in her emptiness
Then the antiworld
Holds the little box in its antihand

Who will bite off the antiworld's antihand
And on that hand
Five hundred antifingers

Do you believe
You'll bite it off
With your thirty-two teeth

Or are you waiting
For the little box
To fly into your mouth

Is this why you are staring

The Prisoners of
the Little Box

Open little box

We kiss your bottom and cover
Keyhole and key

The entire world lies crumpled in you
It resembles everything
Except itself

Not even a clear-sky mother
Would recognize it any more

The rust will eat your key
Our world and us there inside
And finally you too

We kiss your four sides
And four corners
And twenty-four nails
And anything else you have

Open little box

Last News about the Little Box

The little box which contains the world
Fell in love with herself
And conceived
Still another little box

The little box of the little box
Also fell in love with herself
And conceived
Still another little box

And so it went on forever

The world from the little box
Ought to be inside
The last box of the little box

But not one of the little boxes
Inside the little box in love with herself
Is the last one

Let's see you find the world now

ITALO CALVINO

Cities & Desire 5

From there, after six days and seven nights, you arrive at Zobeide, the white city, well exposed to the moon, with streets wound about themselves as in a skein. They tell this tale of its foundation: men of various nations had an identical dream. They saw a woman running at night through an unknown city; she was seen from behind, with long hair, and she was naked. They dreamed of pursuing her. As they twisted and turned, each of them lost her. After the dream they set out in search of that city; they never found it, but they found one another; they decided to build a city like the one in the dream. In laying out the streets, each followed the course of his pursuit; at the spot where they had lost the fugitive's trail, they arranged spaces and walls differently from the dream, so she would be unable to escape again.

This was the city of Zobeide, where they settled, waiting for that scene to be repeated one night. None of them, asleep or awake, ever saw the woman again. The city's streets were streets where they went to work every day, with no link any more to the dreamed chase. Which, for that matter, had long been forgotten.

New men arrived from other lands, having had a dream like theirs, and in the city of Zobeide, they recognized something of the streets of the dream, and they changed the positions of arcades and stairways to resemble more closely the path of the pursued woman so, at the spot where she had vanished, there would remain no avenue of escape.

The first to arrive could not understand what drew these people to Zobeide, this ugly city, this trap.

Hidden Cities 1

In Olinda, if you go out with a magnifying glass and hunt carefully, you may find somewhere a point no bigger than the head of a pin which, if you look at it slightly enlarged, reveals within itself the roofs, the antennas, the skylights, the gardens, the pools, the streamers across the streets, the kiosks in the squares, the horse-racing track. That point does not remain there: a year later you will find it the size of half a lemon, then as large as a mushroom, then a soup plate. And then it becomes a full-size city, enclosed within the earlier city: a new city that forces its way ahead in the earlier city and presses it toward the outside.

Olinda is certainly not the only city that grows in concentric circles, like tree trunks which each year add one more ring. But in other cities there remains, in the center, the old narrow girdle of the walls from which the withered spires rise, the towers, the tiled roofs, the domes, while the new quarters sprawl around them like a loosened belt. Not Olinda: the old walls expand bearing the old quarters with them, enlarged, but maintaining their proportions on a broader horizon at the edges of the city; they surround the slightly newer quarters, which also grew up on the margins and became thinner to make room for still more recent ones pressing from inside; and so, on and on, to the heart of the city, a totally new Olinda which, in its reduced dimensions retains the features and the flow of lymph of the first Olinda and of all the Olindas that have blossomed one from the other; and within this innermost circle there are already blossoming—though it is hard to discern them— the next Olinda and those that will grow after it.

Cities & Signs 1

You walk for days among trees and among stones. Rarely does the eye light on a thing, and then only when it has recognized that thing as the sign of another thing: a print in the sand indicates the tiger's passage; a marsh announces a vein of water; the hibiscus flower, the end of winter. All the rest is silent and interchangeable; trees and stones are only what they are.

Finally the journey leads to the city of Tamara. You penetrate it along streets thick with signboards jutting from the walls. The eye does not see things but images of things that mean other things: pincers point out the tooth-drawer's house; a tankard, the tavern; halberds, the barracks; scales, the grocer's. Statues and shields depict lions, dolphins, towers, stars: a sign that something—who knows what?—has as its sign a lion or a dolphin or a tower or a star. Other signals warn of what is forbidden in a given place (to enter the alley with wagons, to urinate behind the kiosk, to fish with your pole from the bridge) and what is allowed (watering zebras, playing bowls, burning relatives' corpses). From the doors of the temples the gods' statues are seen, each portrayed with his attributes—the cornucopia, the hourglass, the medusa—so that the worshiper can recognize them and address his prayers correctly. If a building has no signboard or figure, its very form and the position it occupies in the city's order suffice to indicate its function: the palace, the prison, the mint, the Pythagorean school, the brothel. The wares, too, which the vendors display on their stalls are valuable not in themselves but as signs of other things: the embroidered headband stands for elegance; the gilded palanquin, power; the volumes of Averroës, learning; the ankle bracelet, voluptuousness. Your gaze scans the streets as if they were written pages: the city says everything you must think, makes you repeat her discourse, and while you believe you are visiting Tamara you are only recording the names with which she defines herself and all her parts.

However the city may really be, beneath this thick coating of signs, whatever it may contain or conceal, you leave Tamara without having discovered it. Outside, the land stretches, empty, to the horizon; the sky opens, with speeding clouds. In the shape that chance and wind give the clouds, you are already intent on recognizing figures: a sailing ship, a hand, an elephant. . . .

Cities & Signs 2

Travelers return from the city of Zirma with distinct memories: a blind black man shouting in the crowd, a lunatic teetering on a skyscraper's cornice, a girl walking with a puma on a leash. Actually many of the blind men who tap their canes on Zirma's cobblestones are black; in every skyscraper there is someone going mad; all lunatics spend hours on cornices; there is no puma that some girl does not raise, as a whim. The city is redundant: it repeats itself so that something will stick in the mind.

I too am returning from Zirma: my memory includes dirigibles flying in all directions, at window level; streets of shops where tattoos are drawn on sailors' skin; underground trains crammed with obese women suffering from the humidity. My traveling companions, on the other hand, swear they saw only one dirigible hovering among the city's spires, only one tattoo artist arranging needles and inks and pierced patterns on his bench, only one fat woman fanning herself on a train's platform. Memory is redundant: it repeats signs so that the city can begin to exist.

Trading Cities 1

Proceeding eighty miles into the northwest wind, you reach the city of Euphemia, where the merchants of seven nations gather at every solstice and equinox. The boat that lands there with a cargo of ginger and cotton will set sail again, its hold filled with pistachio nuts and poppy seeds, and the caravan that has just unloaded sacks of nutmegs and raisins is already cramming its saddlebags with bolts of golden muslin for the return journey. But what drives men to travel up rivers and cross deserts to come here is not only the exchange of wares, which you could find, everywhere the same, in all the bazaars inside and outside the Great Khan's empire, scattered at your feet on the same yellow mats, in the shade of the same awnings protecting them from the flies, offered with the same lying reduction in prices. You do not come to Euphemia only to buy and sell, but also because at night, by the fires all around the market, seated on sacks or barrels or stretched out on piles of carpets, at each word that one man says—such as "wolf," "sister," "hidden treasure," "battle," "scabies," "lovers"—the others tell, each one, his tale of wolves, sisters, treasures, scabies, lovers, battles. And you know that in the long journey ahead of you, when to keep awake against the camel's swaying or the junk's rocking, you start summoning up your memories one by one, your wolf will have become another wolf, your sister a different sister, your battle other battles, on your return from Euphemia, the city where memory is traded at every solstice and at every equinox.

Cities & Signs 5

No one, wise Kublai, knows better than you that the city must never be confused with the words that describe it. And yet between the one and the other there is a connection. If I describe to you Olivia, a city rich in products and in profits, I can indicate its prosperity only by speaking of filigree palaces with fringed cushions on the seats by the mullioned windows. Beyond the screen of a patio, spinning jets water a lawn where a white peacock spreads its tail. But from these words you realize at once how Olivia is shrouded in a cloud of soot and grease that sticks to the houses, that in the brawling streets, the shifting trailers crush pedestrians against the walls. If I must speak to you of the inhabitants' industry, I speak of the saddlers' shops smelling of leather, of the women chattering as they weave raffia rugs, of the hanging canals whose cascades move the paddles of the mills; but the image these words evoke in your enlightened mind is of the mandrel set against the teeth of the lathe, an action repeated by thousands of hands thousands of times at the pace established for each shift. If I must explain to you how Olivia's spirit tends toward a free life and a refined civilization, I will tell you of ladies who glide at night in illuminated canoes between the banks of a green estuary; but it is only to remind you that on the outskirts where men and women land every evening like lines of sleepwalkers, there is always someone who bursts out laughing in the darkness, releasing the flow of jokes and sarcasm.

This perhaps you do not know: that to talk of Olivia, I could not use different words. If there really were an Olivia of mullioned windows and peacocks, of saddlers and rug-weavers and canoes and estuaries, it would be a wretched, black, fly-ridden hole, and to describe it, I would have to fall back on the metaphors of soot, the creaking of wheels, repeated actions, sarcasm. Falsehood is never in words; it is in things.

Cities & the Dead 3

No city is more inclined than Eusapia to enjoy life and flee care. And to make the leap from life to death less abrupt, the inhabitants have constructed an identical copy of their city, underground. All corpses, dried in such a way that the skeleton remains sheathed in yellow skin, are carried down there, to continue their former activities. And, of these activities, it is their carefree moments that take first place: most of the corpses are seated around laden tables, or placed in dancing positions, or made to play little trumpets. But all the trades and professions of the living Eusapia are also at work below ground, or at least those that the living performed with more contentment than irritation: the clockmaker, amid all the stopped clocks of his shop, places his parchment ear against an out-of-tune grandfather's clock; a barber, with dry brush, lathers the cheekbones of an actor learning his role, studying the script with hollow sockets; a girl with a laughing skull milks the carcass of a heifer.

To be sure, many of the living want a fate after death different from their lot in life: the necropolis is crowded with big-game hunters, mezzosopranos, bankers, violinists, duchesses, courtesans, generals—more than the living city ever contained.

The job of accompanying the dead down below and arranging them in the desired place is assigned to a confraternity of hooded brothers. No one else has access to the Eusapia of the dead and everything known about it has been learned from them.

They say that the same confraternity exists among the dead and that it never fails to lend a hand; the hooded brothers, after death, will perform the same job in the other Eusapia; rumor has it that some of them are already dead but continue going up and down. In any case, this confraternity's authority in the Eusapia of the living is vast.

They say that every time they go below they find something changed in the lower Eusapia; the dead make innovations in their city; not many, but surely the fruit of sober reflection, not passing whims. From one year to the next, they say, the Eusapia of the dead becomes unrecognizable. And the living, to keep up with them, also want to do everything that the hooded brothers tell them about the novelties of the dead. So the Eusapia of the living has taken to copying its underground copy.

They say that this has not just now begun to happen: actually it was the dead who built the upper Eusapia, in the image of their city. They say that in the twin cities there is no longer any way of knowing who is alive and who is dead.

Continuous Cities 4

You reproach me because each of my stories takes you right into the heart of a city without telling you of the space that stretches between one city and the other, whether it is covered by seas, or fields of rye, larch forests, swamps. I will answer you with a story.

In the streets of Cecilia, an illustrious city, I met once a goatherd, driving a tinkling flock along the walls.

"Man blessed by heaven," he asked me, stopping, "can you tell me the name of the city in which we are?"

"May the gods accompany you!" I cried. "How can you fail to recognize the illustrious city of Cecilia?"

"Bear with me," that man answered. "I am a wandering herdsman. Sometimes my goats and I have to pass through cities; but we are unable to distinguish them. Ask me the names of the grazing lands, I know them all: the Meadow between the Cliffs, the Green Slope, the Shadowed Grass. Cities have no name for me: they are places without leaves, separating one pasture from another, and where the goats are frightened at street corners and scatter. The dog and I run to keep the flock together."

"I am the opposite of you," I said. "I recognize only cities and cannot distinguish what is outside them. In uninhabited places each stone and each clump of grass mingles, in my eyes, with every other stone and clump."

Many years have gone by since then; I have known many more cities and I have crossed continents. One day I was walking among rows of identical houses; I was lost. I asked a passerby: "May the immortals protect you, can you tell me where we are?"

"In Cecilia, worse luck!" he answered. "We have been wandering through its streets, my goats and I, for an age, and we cannot find our way out. . . ."

I recognized him, despite his long white beard; it was the same herdsman of long before. He was followed by a few, mangy goats, which did not even stink, they were so reduced to skin-and-bones. They cropped wastepaper in the rubbish bins.

"That cannot be!" I shouted. "I, too, entered a city, I cannot remember when, and since then I have gone on, deeper and deeper into its streets. But how have I managed to arrive where you say, when I was in another city, far far away from Cecilia, and I have not yet left it?"

"The places have mingled," the goatherd said. "Cecila is everywhere. Here, once upon a time, there must have been the Meadow of the Low Sage. My goats recognize the grass on the traffic island."

Cities & the Sky 5

Those who arrive at Thekla can see little of the city, beyond the plank fences, the sackcloth screens, the scaffoldings, the metal armatures, the wooden catwalks hanging from ropes or supported by sawhorses, the ladders, the trestles. If you ask, "Why is Thekla's construction taking such a long time?" the inhabitants continue hoisting sacks, lowering leaded strings, moving long brushes up and down, as they answer, "So that its destruction cannot begin." And if asked whether they fear that, once the scaffoldings are removed, the city may begin to crumble and fall to pieces, they add hastily, in a whisper, "Not only the city."

If, dissatisfied with the answers, someone puts his eye to a crack in a fence, he sees cranes pulling up other cranes, scaffoldings that embrace other scaffoldings, beams that prop up other beams. "What meaning does your construction have?" he asks. "What is the aim of a city under construction unless it is a city? Where is the plan you are following, the blueprint?"

"We will show it to you as soon as the working day is over; we cannot interrupt our work now," they answer.

Work stops at sunset. Darkness falls over the building site. The sky is filled with stars. "There is the blueprint," they say.

CONTRIBUTORS

YEHUDA AMICHAI (1924). Born in Germany. Emigrated to Israel in 1936. A poet and novelist, he lives and teaches in Jerusalem. His novel *Not of This Time, Not of This Place* was translated into English. Michael Hamburger says: "It is his acute historical consciousness that makes Amichai's poems at once tragic and humorous, tender and tough, direct and intricate." *Yehuda Amichai: Selected Poems* (1968), *Poems* (1969), *Selected Poems* (1971), and *Songs of Jerusalem and Myself* (1973).

JOHANNES BOBROWSKI (1917–1965). East German poet and novelist. Began writing in early 1940s but did not become available in print and known until 1960s, when his poems received immediate and wide acclaim. At that time he was translated into many European languages and given a number of important literary prizes. Bobrowski's poems are to be found in two volumes: *Shadow Land* (1966) and *Johannes Bobrowski / Horst Bienek* (1971).

ITALO CALVINO (1923). Italian novelist and short-story writer. Took part in the resistance movement. Studied arts. Has worked as an editor since 1947. He moves from the early neo-realism of his fiction to progressively more visionary and surrealistic stories which have the conciseness and lyricism of prose poems. His books are: *The Path to the Nest of Spiders* (1956), *Adam One Afternoon* (1957), *The Non-Existent Knight* (1959), *Baron in the Trees* (1959), *Cosmicomics* (1969), *t zero* (1969), *The Watcher and Other Stories* (1971), and *Invisible Cities* (1974).

PAUL CELAN (1920–1970). Born in Rumania. His parents were murdered by the Nazis and he was sent to a labor camp. Although he wrote in German, he was a French citizen and lived most of his life in France. Celan translated Rimbaud, Valery, Blok, Yesenin, and Mandelstam. His early poetry is influenced by surrealism and expressionism, and the later work has a unique, nearly hermetic idiom where attention to language and its content is the ruling obsession. *Selected Poems* (1972), *Speech-Grille* (1971), and *Nineteen Poems* (1973).

JULIO CORTÁZAR (1914). Argentine novelist, short-story writer, and literary critic. Has lived most of his life in Paris, where he works as a translator for UNESCO. Influenced by Borges, Kafka, and perhaps Michaux. Cortázar is a profoundly experimental writer. What makes his visions powerful is that the surreal and the miraculous occur in the midst of ordinary life. They have, for his protagonists, both intellectual and tragic implications. The selection in this anthology comes out of his book *Cronopios and Famas* (1968). His other works in English: *The Winners* (1965), *Hopscotch* (1966), *The End of the Game and Other Stories* (1967), *All Fires the Fire* (1973), *Sixty-two: A Model Kit* (1972).

CARLOS DRUMMOND DE ANDRADE (1902). Brazilian poet and short-story writer. Lives in Rio de Janeiro where, until his retirement in 1966, he was a civil servant in the Ministry of Education. A master of the plain style, he has deliberately carried the Modernist revolt against traditional poetic rhetoric one step further. His poems are ironic, compassionate meditations on the fugitive and ephemeral character of experience. Some of his poems about his childhood in Minas Gerais can be found in *An Anthology of Twentieth Century Brazilian Poetry* (1972). The only whole book devoted to a selection of his poems is *In the Middle of the Road* (1965).

JEAN FOLLAIN (1903–1971). Associated with Max Jacob, Pierre Reverdy, and Leon-Paul Fargue. Practiced law and was a magistrate until 1959. A poet of deceiving simplicity and subtle effects, Follain has the ability to restore the most commonplace event to its strangeness and endow it with an almost cosmic resonance. In that sense his poems are truly visionary, and his art that of a patient, sly craftsman. There is one volume in English: *Transparence of the World* (1969).

ZBIGNIEW HERBERT (1924). The best Polish poet of his generation. Participated in the resistance movement during World War II. Studied economics, law, and philosophy. Has traveled a great deal since and worked at various jobs. An erudite poet with a fine sense of the Western intellectual tradition. His poems are restrained, often ironic meditations on history. His *Selected Poems* were published in English in 1968.

MIROSLAV HOLUB (1923). Czech poet. A well-known research scientist. Spent 1966–1967 in the United States. Close to Parra in his dislike of traditional rhetoric. Holub wants a poetry that "ordinary people can read as naturally as they read the papers, or go to a football game." The two volumes in English are: *Selected Poems* (1967) and *Although* (1971).

HENRI MICHAUX (1899). Belgian poet and painter. Michaux has traveled all over the world, has experimented with drugs, and has written extensively about these experiences. His literary ancestors are Swift, Rabelais, Voltaire, the journals of early explorers, the medieval bestiaries. For sheer invention and imaginative range he is unequaled in this century. Available in English are: *A Barbarian in Asia* (1949), *A Miserable Miracle* (1963), *Selected Writings* (1968), *Ecuador* (1970), and *The Major Ordeals of the Mind* (1974).

CZESLAW MILOSZ (1911). Polish poet, essayist, and novelist. Fought in the underground during World War II. After several years in the diplomatic service, he severed his ties with the new government and became an exile. Presently lives and teaches at the University of California, Berkeley. Milosz is one of the major poets of this century. His poetry, with its clear sense of history and of himself as a participant and a victim, communicates perhaps better than any other what it means to live in this age. His books in English are: *The Captive Mind* (1954), *Postwar Polish Poetry: An Anthology* (1965 / 1970), *Native Realm: A Search for a Definition* (1968), *Selected Poems of Zbigniew Herbert*, translated with Peter Dale Scott (1968), *The History of Polish Literature* (1969), *Selected Poems* (1973).

NICANOR PARRA (1914). Chilean poet. Professor of mathematics and physics. Studied in United States and England. His second book, *Poems and Antipoems*, published in 1954, introduced the term "antipoetry." Parra's antipoetry is a gesture against traditional poetic rhetoric and its sentimental cosmology. Deliberately flat, conversational, and ironic, his poems nevertheless have a genuine and unique lyrical quality. Available in English: *Antipoems* (1960), *Poems and Antipoems* (1967), *Emergency Poems* (1972).

OCTAVIO PAZ (1914). Mexican poet and essayist. In Europe in 1937 he met Neruda, Vallejo, Hernandez, and the French surrealists. In Mexican foreign service in various capacities. Lived in San Francisco, New York, Paris, Tokyo, Geneva, and Delhi. In 1968 resigned his ambassadorship in India in protest against Mexican government's harsh treatment of demonstrating students. An eclectic writer. His interests range over the entire landscape of contemporary literature, philosophy, arts, and psychology. The main thrust of his poetry and thinking, however, is toward his cultural roots and Mexican identity. Many of his books have been translated into English: *The Labyrinth of Solitude* (1962), *Sun Stone* (1963), *Selected Poems* (1963), *Marcel Duchamp or the Castle of Purity* (1970), *Aguila o sol?—Eagle or Sun?* (1970), *Configurations* (1971), *The Other Mexico: Critique of the Pyramid* (1972), *Alternating Current* (1973), *The Bow and the Lyre* (1973), *Conjunctions and Disjunctions* (1974), and *Children of the Mire* (1974).

FERNANDO PESSOA (1888–1933). Generally regarded as the greatest Portuguese poet since Camões. Wrote under three pseudonyms, three contradictory sides of himself: Alvaro de Campos, a follower of Whitman; Ricardo Reis, a classical pastoral poet; Alberto Caeiro, an intellectual and antipoet. It has been pointed out that all of Pessoa's work is a search for lost identity. As he says, "I put into Caeiro all my power of dramatic depersonalization, into Ricardo Reis all my intellectual discipline, dressed in a music that is proper to him, into Alvaro de Campos all the emotion that I do not allow myself in living. To think . . . that all these must be, in the act of publication, overtakers of Fernando Pessoa, impure and simple!" In English: *Selected Poems* (1971), and *Sixty Portuguese Poems* (1973).

FRANCIS PONGE (1899). French. Has been a journalist, a teacher, and a publisher. Although he has rejected being called a poet, his highly original, almost phenomenological meditations on inanimate objects have had a great deal of influence on recent French poetry and fiction. Both structuralists and *nouveau roman* have claimed him as one of their own. Ponge's work has been translated for years in magazines and is now available in English in the following volumes: *Soap* (1969), *Things* (1971), and *The Voices of Things* (1972).

VASKO POPA (1922). Yugoslav poet. Originally influenced by French surrealism. His own unique idiom has its basis in Serbian folklore. Popa's poems are written in cycles, each one proceeding in a series of archetypal dialectical gestures around a common point of reference. The impulse is toward the epic and has a great intellectual range. Most of his poems have been translated: *Selected Poems* (1969), *The Little Box* (1970), *Earth Erect* (1973).

YANNIS RITSOS (1909). Greek author of over forty volumes of poetry and translations. Imprisoned for long periods of time for his leftist politics. His books were banned in Greece by the military dictatorship. A superb lyric poet of an almost classical purity, Ritsos has an excellence and range can be only hinted at in a selection such as this one. In English: *Gestures* (1971).